"*Stage (Not Age)* is your own personal master class for understanding, entering, and thriving in the fast-growing, $22 trillion longevity market. The profiles of companies that successfully serve this market will cause you to rethink everything you thought you knew about aging."

—**JO ANN JENKINS,** CEO, AARP

"We can continue viewing the aging of the world's population as an imminent crisis, or we can choose to see it as an opportunity for business and policy innovations, for advancing and improving people's health and lives at an older age. This book guides us toward the latter view, and brilliantly."

—**MICHELLE A. WILLIAMS,** Dean of the Faculty, Harvard T.H. Chan
   School of Public Health

"People, like wine, get better with age. Our aging society offers extraordinary opportunities for businesses, as Susan Golden's important book demonstrates. While some complain about the costs of an older population, *Stage (Not Age)* offers a thoughtful roadmap for understanding the ways in which the fastest-growing demographic can drive value."

—**LARRY SUMMERS,** President, Emeritus, Harvard University; former
   Secretary of the Treasury of the United States

"We're living through an extraordinary demographic transition. Susan Golden's book offers an inspiring roadmap for entrepreneurs and innovators to grow with the longevity economy."

—**JONATHAN LEVIN,** Dean, Stanford Graduate School of Business

"An insightful and practical guide to an amazing and multifaceted business. *Stage (Not Age)* is the indispensable guide for companies to develop a strategy for this opportunity—as we did at Best Buy."

—**HUBERT JOLY,** former Chairman and CEO, Best Buy; author, *The Heart
   of Business*; and senior lecturer, Harvard Business School

"In *Stage (Not Age)*, Susan Golden makes an eloquent case for investing in one of the most compelling business opportunities of our time—the multigenerational society already transforming all aspects of our lives. Her book is a clearly written, insightful guide. A must-read for changemakers of all ages."

—**MARC FREEDMAN,** founder, President, and CEO, Encore.org; author, *How to Live Forever*

"How do you reach a generation (or two) of people who don't feel, look, or act as old as they are? By not focusing on the number on their birth certificate and instead focusing on those thoughts, feelings, and actions. That's the message of Susan Wilner Golden's enlightening new book. Companies and marketers willing to listen should find themselves at an advantage."

—**JEAN CHATZKY,** CEO, HerMoney Media; *New York Times* bestselling coauthor, *AgeProof*

STAGE
(Not Age)

SUSAN WILNER GOLDEN

STAGE
(Not Age)

HOW TO UNDERSTAND AND SERVE
PEOPLE OVER 60—THE FASTEST
GROWING, MOST DYNAMIC
MARKET IN THE WORLD

HARVARD BUSINESS REVIEW PRESS
BOSTON, MASSACHUSETTS

Library of Congress Cataloging-in-Publication Data
Names: Golden, Susan (Susan Wilner), author.
  Title: Stage (not age) : how to understand and serve people over 60, the
    fastest growing, most dynamic market in the world / Susan Golden.
  Description: Boston, Massachusetts : Harvard Business Review Press, [2022] |
    Includes index.
  Identifiers: LCCN 2022004499 (print) | LCCN 2022004500 (ebook) |
    ISBN 9781633699472 (hardcover) | ISBN 9781633699489 (epub)
  Subjects: LCSH: Older consumers. | Population aging. | Cohort analysis. |
    Success in business.
  Classification: LCC HQ1061 .G64185 2022 (print) | LCC HQ1061 (ebook) |
    DDC 305.26—dc23/eng/20220210
  LC record available at https://lccn.loc.gov/2022004499
  LC ebook record available at https://lccn.loc.gov/2022004500
    ISBN: 978-1-63369-947-2
    eISBN: 978-1-63369-948-9

To Amanda, Jenny, and David,
who have given me the gifts of joy and laughter—
my own personal prescription for longevity

and

To my extraordinary parents,
whose courage and resilience continue to
inspire me every day

CONTENTS

STAGE
(Not Age)

A New Demographic Reality

One hundred years old.

There's something about that marker, a century. It's a simple number. Easy to grasp as a real milestone for a life. For a long time, it was so rare that it was celebrated. People who reached one hundred were newsworthy. Just a hundred years ago, the average American could expect to live fifty-four years. By the end of World War II, it was sixty-four. When the personal computer debuted in 1981, life expectancy had reached seventy-four. Today it's nearly eighty, and in one generation, public health and medical advances will enable children born since 2000 to expect to live to one hundred; adults like me who arrive at good health at age sixty-five have better-than-even odds of living well into their nineties. This new longevity is one of the most remarkable achievements of the twentieth and early twenty-first centuries.

It also radically shifts the demographic profile of this country and nearly every other country on the planet. Soon, older people will outnumber younger people virtually everywhere except Africa. More than ten thousand people are turning sixty-five each day in the United States. In Japan—the oldest country in the world—a full third of the population is over sixty-five, by far the highest proportion of any country.

These demographic changes are known and inevitable. Experts have been talking about this issue in public policy circles for years, primarily as a potential crisis or at least as a shift that needs to be prepared for. But I'm here to talk about this demographic fact as an enormous business and market opportunity. There is a new longevity customer. A new longevity employee. A new longevity entrepreneur. And a new longevity economy, estimated at more than $22 trillion worldwide (in the United States, $8.3 trillion). As we consider the needs, opportunities, and desires related to a hundred-plus-year life, we aim to enhance not just longevity but also what is called *healthspan*—the number of years that people live well.

The tectonic demographic shift must be met with a similarly immense mindset shift. Our long-held presumptions, heuristics, and approaches to understanding what it means to be old and to serve this cohort no longer apply. Sixty-five as an age marker that signifies the entry into old age no longer works. The classic view of modern life was one of three stages: learn, earn, retire. No more. It doesn't make sense anymore. You don't retire at sixty-five if you have 35 percent of your life left. A greater number of people in this age range means there will be much more diversity—literal diversity, yes, but also diversity in what people do in this time, what they need, what they want, and how they age.

Older adults have always been defined—culturally and as a market—by their age. It's time to stop that and think instead about the *stage* older adults find themselves in as the most important attribute. To understand the swelling ranks of people over sixty-five is to recognize stage, not age.

For example, multiple life stages now exist within retirement, including more learning and earning. Also there are septuagenarian entrepreneurs and people in their sixties starting new careers. This book will help you understand this new reality and help you serve the many stages in this growing, dynamic demographic of what we used to call old people. I will describe a new paradigm that captures the many stages at multiple ages that people will experience—what I call the five quarters, or 5Qs. To understand and serve this massive market, you will have to think in fresh ways about, say, continuous learners in their eighties and nineties. You have to think simultaneously about different profiles of caregivers for older adults: those caregivers may either be thirty-year-olds or those in their seventies and eighties. You must realize that there will no longer be an age of full retirement but that there will be a great repurposing instead. Most vitally, you have to break your long-held beliefs of what it means when you hear that someone is eighty-two years old. Even within a single age range, you will find marvelous diversity and huge new opportunities.

$$\bullet \quad \bullet \quad \bullet$$

As I was in the middle of writing this book, the Covid-19 pandemic overtook our communities, our health-care system, our educational system, our work, our families, and the rest of our lives. Much of the optimism I exude in the book is based on starting this project before the pandemic, when the idea that a virus would shift demographics wasn't even a thought. Then, life expectancy was shortened in 2020, in part because certain important public health measures were initially delayed. Covid-19 infections were the third leading cause of death in the United States in 2020, and at the end of 2021, over eight hundred thousand deaths have occurred—the vast majority among those over sixty-five. It will continue to affect our story until vaccination rates achieve the levels similar to those achieved with the polio vaccine. Meanwhile, we cannot know how long Covid-19 will be in our communities, when the pandemic will end, or when we will feel the same sense of normal that defined our pre-pandemic lifestyles.

It was predominantly public health measures that enabled us to realize the opportunity to live to one hundred. It will be a continued devotion to public health that will get us past the pandemic, provided we adhere to public health recommendations and the longevity prescription that I advocate for in this book: purpose, wellness, and community.

In spite of its true awfulness, Covid-19 has been a catalyst for the changes needed. The pandemic has forced us to reexamine everything in a way that we in the longevity community had already started to do: work, transportation, housing, health care, and social connections, to name a few. People are asking the questions we've been asking: How will work change? How will education have to change? How should communities and countries help people live securely? And how will businesses integrate these changes and opportunities into their strategy?

People are talking about many of the issues we have too long ignored: caregiving, end of life, working longer, and working remotely. Living and dying with dignity has become a national conversation and one that should influence how you think about the longevity customer you want to help. Companies should be investing in dignity. While painful at times, these conversations are critical.

Innovations created during the pandemic will be integrated more permanently. Stores created shopping hours for those over sixty. New startups emerged to help provide food and tech support to the aging population. Telehealth was meaningfully integrated into health-care delivery and is opening up many new business opportunities.

Finally, culturally, we came to recognize the contributions of older adults and the value they bring to society both in times of crisis and in prosperity. This value was most eloquently illustrated during the pandemic by leaders such as Anthony Fauci and retired nurses and doctors, all of whom came to the front lines and contributed in essential ways.

• • •

So, my pre-pandemic optimism remains in the following pages, albeit in a way that acknowledges the challenges ahead given the world-shaking events of 2020 and 2021.

The $22 trillion opportunity is still there. This book will help you— the companies, innovators, marketers, entrepreneurs, investors, and older adults—reimagine the opportunities and implications presented by the new longevity. It aims to help you understand and serve people over sixty, the fastest-growing, most dynamic market in the world.

I've organized the book into two parts. Part 1 focuses on understanding longevity and shifting your mindset to thinking about older adults by the stage of life they're in, not by the number that tells you how old they are.

Chapter 1 sets the table by explaining changing demographics and the distinction between lifespan (an age concept) and healthspan (a stage concept). Chapter 2 resets the discussion around longevity by reinventing the language around it. It has become meaningless to describe someone as merely "old," and it's even more damaging to use terms like *elderly.* New terms and new narratives are needed, and I provide them with my 5Q life framework: a new way to view this part of life not as a single march to the sunset but rather as a portfolio of activities all happening at the same time. Chapter 3 summarizes the practical segmentation of the longevity market and settles on some key segments to explore further. All these segments are not focused on how old the customer is but rather consider what stages they fit into.

Part 2 will then dive into the opportunities in this market and the roadblocks you should anticipate and overcome. Chapter 4 profiles companies that have identified a successful longevity strategy and identifies growing opportunities that you may not have considered for the over-sixty market. Chapter 5 details the different types of longevity customers, including purchasers and payers who may not be the end users of your product or service, and the varied customer acquisition challenges you might encounter. Chapter 6 lays out the channel and distribution challenges you're sure to face and some emerging platforms to address them. An overview of the emerging entrepreneurship opportunities, both for and by older adults, is outlined in chapter 7.

The book concludes in chapter 8 with a call to arms on being an active participant in changing the conversation about older adults, addressing ageism, fostering intergenerational communities and opportunities for innovation, supporting policies that will effect change, and investing in dignity.

While all this material is important, some chapters may be more useful to you than others; they may be ones you refer to again and again as you develop your strategy. Maybe you are focused on the entrepreneurship opportunity, for example. To make the book as practical as possible for all readers, I provide both a summary of the big idea at the beginning of the chapter and a list of key takeaways at the end. Many chapters will include more material than you can use when adopting your own longevity strategy. I hope this practical approach aids you in your journey.

Each new company, new business strategy, and new solution that will address the needs of older adults can have a major impact on your customers, employees, and community. When you can address these needs you're improving society as a whole. I hope that in these pages, you find your own longevity opportunity to help people enjoy better, more secure, and longer lives filled with dignity.

PART ONE

UNDERSTANDING LONGEVITY

CHAPTER 1

From Lifespan to Healthspan

Population aging, fueled by declining birth rates and increases in life expectancy, is a megatrend that will continue in the United States and many other countries for the next several decades.[1] The doubling of lifespans in the past century and a half is one of the most remarkable success stories in human history. Over half of children now being born are expected to live to age one hundred and beyond. Every business needs to develop its strategy for the opportunities presented by the new longevity.

Understanding the opportunity in front of you with the market of older adults begins with a deeper understanding of the demographic shift underway and the first mindset shift it requires, from thinking about lifespan to healthspan.

Here's a timeline of the major demographic shifts both underway and in the near future:[2]

- 2020: Some 35 percent of the US population is over sixty-five (111 million people); over 10,000 baby boomers turn sixty-five every day in the United States.

- 2035: People over sixty-five will outnumber people under eighteen in the United States.

- 2050: Around 45 percent of the US population will be older than sixty-five, and people eighty and older are 8 percent of the population and the fastest-growing segment; people over sixty-five will outnumber people younger than fifteen for the first time in human history.

- 2050: Some 3.2 billion people worldwide are older than fifty (1.6 billion today).

The crossover from old to young, i.e., the percentage of people under eighteen and those sixty-five and older, can be starkly visualized. The switch from old to young is about a decade away (figure 1-1).[3] And in the century between 1960 and 2060, the United States will transform from a young country with a rapidly tapering proportion of people over thirty-five to a country with thick, even bands of people all the way to seventy-five years old.[4] Only after that do the proportions taper, and then only a little bit.

Longevity versus Aging

To talk meaningfully about demographic changes, we should pay particular attention to the lexicon we use. In chapter 2, we'll tackle words and their role in shaping people's perception and understanding of this demographic, including ageism. For now, we have to distinguish between some basic, often-confused terms if we are to understand the opportunity ahead.

People often confuse longevity with aging. Marking a ninetieth birthday tells us everything about a person's longevity but nothing about their aging. *Longevity* is the length of lifespan, independent of the biological process of aging. Whereas longevity is chronological, aging is completely biological and is a natural phenomenon. It is the process of progressive, event-dependent decline in the ability to maintain biochemical and physiological function. Aging drives increased risk of disease and mortality. Nearly every major fatal disease in developed

FIGURE 1-1

Projected numbers of children and older adults in the United States, 2016 to 2060

For the first time in US history, older adults are projected to outnumber children by 2035.

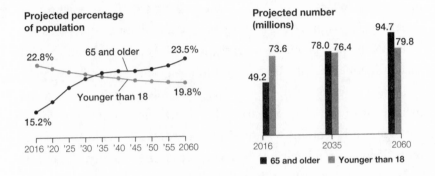

Projected percentage of population

22.8%   65 and older   23.5%

15.2%

Younger than 18   19.8%

2016 '20 '25 '30 '35 '40 '45 '50 '55 2060

Projected number (millions)

| | 73.6 | 78.0 76.4 | 94.7 79.8 |
| 49.2 | | | |

2016   2035   2060

■ 65 and older   ■ Younger than 18

Population of the United States

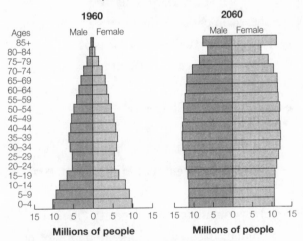

1960

Ages   Male Female

85+
80–84
75–79
70–74
65–69
60–64
55–59
50–54
45–49
40–44
35–39
30–34
25–29
20–24
15–19
10–14
5–9
0–4

15 10 5 0 5 10 15

Millions of people

2060

Male Female

15 10 5 0 5 10 15

Millions of people

Source: US Census Bureau, "An Aging Nation: Projected Number of Children and Adults," Census Infographics and Visualizations, March 13, 2018, www.census.gov/library/visualizations/2018/comm/historic-first.html; and US Census Bureau, "From Pyramid to Pillar: A Century of Change, Population of the U.S.," Census Info-graphic and Visualizations, March 13, 2018, www.census.gov/library/visualizations/2018/comm/century -of-change.html.

countries shares a common feature: your risk of developing the disease increases dramatically as you age.[5]

When I talk about the longevity opportunity, it is not solely the opportunity to better serve an aging population. Significant research and investment dollars are devoted to diminishing the effects of aging and enhancing aging processes to delay the onset of disease. That focus represents only the biological side of the longevity opportunity. It's a small slice of the market, though great innovation is happening in aging, including a range of caloric restriction protocols, as well as the experimental use of the drug rapamycin. Large investments in these types of antiaging interventions will continue. As you understand this market more deeply, you'll likely hear about groups like Longevity Inc. and the Longevity Fund. Confusingly, though they use the term *longevity*, they exclusively focus on biologic interventions to extend life. They are aging-centric. While these companies attract many investors, this segment of the longevity market is not the primary focus of this book. This book is more broadly focused on longevity writ large.

A good way to think about this distinction is that innovations in aging are designed to increase longevity.

Lifespan versus Healthspan

Lifespan is largely synonymous with longevity. One of the most extraordinary facts in human ingenuity was the doubling of our lifespan in 150 years.

For most of history, people lived no more than one generation. In one century, lifespan has increased more than it did in all other prior years combined (figure 1-2). The average life expectancy for a man born in 1900 in the United States was 47, and for a woman, it was 49. American children born today have an average life expectancy of nearly 80, and over two-thirds can expect to live to 104.[6] Between 1960 and 2015, life expectancy for the US population increased by almost ten years, from 69.7 in 1960 to 79.4 years in 2015.[7] My yet-to-be-born grandchildren will

FIGURE 1-2

Life expectancy for people born between 1770 and 2018

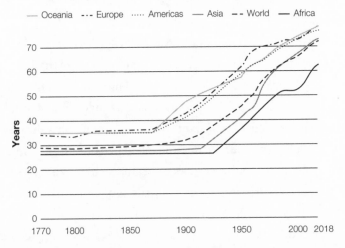

Note: Shown is period life expectancy at birth, the average number of years a newborn would live if the pattern of mortality in the given year were to stay the same through its life.

Source: Data was compiled by Our World in Data based on estimates by James C. Riley, Clio Infra, and the United Nations Population Division. Published online at OurWorldinData.org, https://ourworldindata.org /life-expectancy.

most likely have me around for up to thirty-plus years, and I may well live to enjoy my great-grandchildren.

This astonishing change is the result of a century of increasingly improved public health measures and medical care advances. The twentieth century saw remarkable advances in basic sanitation and medical care, especially during childbirth and infancy. These advances reduced both infant and maternal mortality.

A second major factor has been the control of diseases of childhood through immunizations and antibiotics. More recently, since the 1990s, death rates from the two most common causes of death among Americans, heart disease and cancer, have declined.[8] While these diseases do remain the leading causes of death, people can now live with these chronic conditions much longer.

In the most recent years, increases in life expectancy have slowed and then declined slightly because of the triad of the opioid and obesity epidemics and, of course, the sudden shock of the Covid-19 pandemic. Still, the pandemic has not affected the overall demographic shift: population aging, fueled by declining birth rates and increases in lifespan, is a megatrend that will continue.

But one aspect of this idea of lifespan isn't captured by simple chronology. We must distinguish what's happening now as more than just adding years to lives. People are living longer, yes, but more importantly, they have a longer time living *well*. This period of largely independent and healthy living is what is called a *healthspan*. While definitions vary, healthspan is most commonly expressed as the time that a person is free from the serious diseases that are leading causes of death, such as heart disease, lung cancer, chronic obstructive pulmonary disease, stroke, Alzheimer's disease, type 2 diabetes, colorectal cancer, breast cancer, and prostate cancer.

My own mother's experience well illustrates the difference between lifespan and healthspan. She was an outlier for her generation in that her lifespan was very long; she lived into her nineties. But she did not experience a significantly longer healthspan. Starting in her sixties, she had multiple chronic conditions and endured more than twenty hospitalizations in the last years of her life.

Contrast that with my septuagenarian friend Marc, who recently remarked to me returning from a Maroon 5 rock concert, "My body is seventy. I am forty-five." That's a longer healthspan.

Of course, the healthspan story is more nuanced than just healthy versus unhealthy, and it would be hardly fair to apply this idea to a single giant cohort of all people over sixty, a group comprising tens of millions of people. Not everyone is like Marc, and that's the point. In this three-decade time frame, some individuals may be experiencing the same health status as when they were in their twenties to forties. They may be pursuing a modified portfolio of life activities in their sixties to nineties but may well be working, exercising, traveling, and seeking adventures. One new friend I made in the past five years is an active skier and a race car driver. He runs a major real estate business and in every way is as active as any thirty-five-year-old I know. He is seventy-six.

To take advantage of the longevity opportunity, we must become familiar with the crucial idea of healthspan. Longer healthspans create the diversity of life stages that you will be serving. Healthspans are in fact now considered more important than lifespans.

Although there is a large longevity industry devoted to extended lifespans through drugs and other therapeutics, the greater need and opportunity lie in how to extend people's healthspan and how to serve them as they enjoy more freedom in these years.[9] The distinction is an important one: it is the difference between living to a hundred but spending the last twenty years with a walker or wheelchair and spending the last twenty years walking on the beach or playing tennis. It is the difference between walking to the kitchen and walking to the museum.

Many of the known determinants of healthspan create new opportunities for businesses to consider. It may seem like common sense, but maintaining a healthy, balanced diet with moderate regular exercise and without smoking and drinking large amounts of alcohol is the surest way to promote one's healthspan and limit the onset of diseases. The Mediterranean diet, for one, has fairly broad support in the literature.

Social, intellectual, and physical activities are also huge healthspan determinants. Even though they may be more commonly associated with psychological effects, their strong physiological effects should not be ignored. Social isolation has been determined to have the same deleterious health effects as smoking fifteen cigarettes a day.[10]

Since health is improving and cognitive decline rates are falling, we must eliminate the old stereotypes of how people will age. The data on incidence of dementia shows that the *rates* of new cases are indeed decreasing—suggesting better healthspans. But because of overall increases in longevity, the prevalence is *increasing*. Age-related diseases lower the quality of life for hundreds of thousands of older people and their families. But the vast majority, in fact, will arrive at older age in good health and in the happiest stage of their lives. Already well over half of people eighty-five years old are indeed able to live independently. That happiness increases in older age has been well documented by Laura Carstensen, the founder and director of the Stanford Center on Longevity.[11] Do not fall into the trap that all people over a certain age are declining and waiting out their years till death. In fact, the research shows that the seventies are among the happiest decades that people will enjoy, and with increasing healthspans, those numbers will only improve.

The single greatest determinant of health status in older age is education. This key insight will affect segmentation in the longevity market. (We will examine segmentation in the following chapters.) Education predicts long-term health outcomes more does than any other factor. Equally significant is the impact that education has on income. The number of poor seniors is expected to double to 4.3 million by 2022.[12] Education affects income, which affects your ability to afford good health care, high-quality and nutritious food, housing, and opportunities for maintaining your health through exercise. While we do not yet know the final statistics, preliminary reports of Covid-19 cases suggest that lower incomes and all the factors associated with poverty are associated with higher death rates.

Knowing the factors that contribute to or detract from healthspan will be key to understanding your longevity opportunity and just how deep it goes. But longer lifespans and healthspans clearly create cascading opportunities, and you may try to own all of these opportunities or just play in one segment of them.

For example, Wider Circle was founded in 2015 to address the social isolation that many older people experience by helping them with aging in place. (The company is described in greater detail in chapter 4.) By reducing isolation, the company is increasing people's healthspan. Healthier, less isolated older adults have new services available to them, such as education opportunities (the term *lifelong learning* is becoming literally true). Education opportunities, in turn, open up possibilities in innovating with user experiences for older adults. Innovation then opens up learning platforms and social network possibilities. Hiring older workers is another imperative and innovation opportunity. My friend Evie, who chooses to be a waitress at my favorite breakfast spot in Massachusetts, also works at the local grocery store as a cashier. She does so because it gives her purpose and she wants the social interaction with customers and coworkers instead of retirement.

These simple examples come from just one aspect of the healthspan—social isolation. When you take into consideration all the others, the possibilities increase exponentially.

Longevity + Healthspan = Opportunity

As this demographic upheaval occurs worldwide, longevity in the twenty-first century yields many opportunities for individuals, society, and businesses—yet most people have not begun to think creatively about how longer lives can be a good thing. These insights into demographic changes, the improved health status of aging, and the potential to tap into new and growing markets should encourage all businesses to understand how to address the implications and opportunities of long-lived society and the new old age.

Companies are recognizing the huge implications of longer lifespans and healthspans—as well as the opportunities—in health care, finance, education, housing, and technology. It is a nascent industry. Many new companies are being formed to serve the needs and wants of older adults and to help with end-of-life care and planning. More enterprises are surely needed. However, serving the needs and wants of longer healthspans is different. New products and services will emerge in all domains, including fintech, career and transition planning, health and wellness, intergenerational living and engagement, and leisure and entertainment, to name just a few.

A business response to this opportunity is becoming a mandate for every company, board, leader, entrepreneur, and business school to consider and integrate into its strategy. The longevity sector is, after all, the largest and fastest-growing market. People age fifty and over already account for more than half of consumer spending in the United States and 83 percent of household wealth, with both numbers expected to increase significantly. When has it been a good strategy to ignore such sizable numbers?

Becoming strategic about longevity starts with understanding these demographics and the terms that define the market. Most important, we must understand that the three-stage life of learn, earn, retire, no longer holds and that the increasing healthspans decrease the importance of age in the market. Rather, it will be stage that defines what types of products and services a person will need; how they should be marketed to; who should be marketed to; and how education, work, and career will need to change.

Considerations of stage, not age, to define a customer's needs and wants will become the norm. People between the ages of forty and eighty can conceivably be experiencing the same stage, for example, working, traveling, exercising, and exploring, in good health. A focus on stage will also cause all business sectors, including education, entertainment, clothing, travel, and housing, to consider and develop a new strategy that incorporates the new longevity opportunity.

What Does the Hundred-Year Life Mean to My Business?

For too long, our society has defined many milestones, including when to retire, according to age. The notion of retiring at age sixty-five was introduced back in the 1880s, when human lifespans rarely exceeded age sixty-five. Thus, the US Social Security system was based on that old premise. Today, as people will need to plan for hundred-year lives, retiring at age sixty-five is outdated, given that most people will want and need to work longer. A forty-year workspan can rarely support a forty-year retirement.

Think about that: a generation ago, retiring at age sixty-five was the norm and was viewed as a respite well earned. Today, however, a person retiring at sixty-five is likely to enjoy another thirty-five years of life and, with some effort, thirty-five years of healthspan as well. For many people, that incremental three and one-half decades will be almost as much time as they had already committed to a career, job, or family. People will experience a variety of purposeful and active stages between the traditional retirement age of sixty-five and their end of life, in their nineties or beyond.

There will be novel business opportunities across the lifespan of individuals who can anticipate living to one hundred. Businesses can facilitate career transitions as the nature and length of work changes dramatically. We should expect that a sixty-year education cycle will become the norm instead of the current twenty-year cycle. Becoming and staying an active learner through both work and outside resources will be essential to century-long lives. It is unrealistic to expect an education received in the first twenty years of our lives to support us for the remaining eighty. Financial services firms may rethink the product offerings, including the notion of baby bonds to support the financial needs of longer lives. New housing opportunities will enable people to age in their own home instead of in retirement communities. All these innovations will support longer healthspans as well.

Similarly, the desire to incorporate volunteering, sabbaticals and other career breaks, caregiving leaves, travel, leisure, and intergenerational connections will also become prime components of any business strategy for their workforce. New companies are emerging to help people make the transitions for multiple stages of career and work. Companies that recognize the different stages of life of their employees, and not their age, will thrive.

Increasingly, large companies are offering paid "returnship" programs (programs offering internships to people with more experience) such as Re-Ignite at Johnson & Johnson and reentry programs at J.P. Morgan and Facebook. New companies and programs are being developed to offer opportunities to address the need for ongoing digital literacy among people fifty and older (see chapter 4). Employees may value more types of educational benefits, such as 529 plans for themselves, and not just for their children's education. Being a continuous learner and offering those kinds of opportunities will, I believe, become the norm in century-long lives.

With these longer lives, older people will want to and be able to contribute to the longevity economy in multiple ways themselves. At older ages, they may be employed in full-time or part-time positions; may be self-employed as consultants, contractors, freelancers, or "olderpreneurs";

or may be acting as volunteers or caregivers. All of them will be consumers and will account for a significant redistribution of wealth. Incubators and coworking spaces are now emerging targeting the over-fifty
entrepreneur. Some of these spaces will need to become virtual in a
post-pandemic world as well.

Moreover, most companies have not considered what it will mean to
have a five-generation workforce. Such a workforce will mean, in part,
that there can be more creativity and insights into how different types
of customers, despite being very different ages, may nevertheless be at
similar stages that will factor into product design, consumer services,
and marketing strategies. Longevity-focused companies will ultimately
develop products and services that are multigenerational and appealing
to older consumers.

The value of an experienced workforce is increasingly being recognized and celebrated. These intergenerational workforces will also
afford new opportunities for reverse mentoring and multigenerational
connections. The financial value of multigenerational workforces is also
being better understood. In September 2019, Mercer released its white
paper "Are You Age-Ready?" and its Next Stage platform to help businesses identify the steps for building an age-ready organization.[13] Older
workers add a level of EQ (emotional intelligence) to a workplace and
are not limited to only valuing DQ (digital intelligence). New initiatives
are now underway with AARP and the World Economic Forum to help
businesses recognize these opportunities and take the longevity pledge,
and the Reframing Aging Initiative sponsored by the Gerontological
Society of America as described in chapter 8.

How you consider your own career and life plans in a world of increasing healthspan requires rethinking old norms. You may personally plan for multiple career breaks at different times to focus more on
family, to return for additional educational opportunities, or to take a
sabbatical to reimagine your next stage and chapters. You may rethink
which types of work and career you want to pursue and fully expect to
have as many as six to ten different jobs, without judgment. All this will

occur independent of age but depends much on the stage of life you are experiencing.

You will need to prioritize health and wellness to enhance your own healthspan. You must also be able to lead a multigenerational workforce. A changed mindset in an organization's leadership will help promote an intergenerational workforce, a continuous examination and reexamination of how business strategies could align with the new longevity opportunity, and a renewed commitment to enhancing healthspan and not just lifespan for the twenty-first century. Companies with this mindset are described in further detail in chapter 4. Bring this mindset to your efforts as executives, as product managers, as team leaders, as intrapreneurs (innovators within an organization), and as leaders in your community.

· · ·

The achievement of hundred-year lives during the past century is remarkable. Redesigning the life course for this level of longevity is still in its earliest stages. Longevity is a fact, but that doesn't mean addressing it or seizing on the opportunity is simple. For example, the Stanford Center on Longevity is designing a vision for hundred-year lives and developing its New Map of Life. This multiyear initiative involves researching more flexible models for learning, earning and saving, and how to be longevity ready. In turn, the growing recognition for new approaches to the life course is creating many new opportunities for innovation.[14] The Stanford center asks the important question of when and how we can add in those thirty extra years of lifespan and, ideally, healthspan.

Should these extra thirty years all be used at the end, or should they be interspersed into new and longer stages of life? Should undergraduate education be distributed over a six-year period, with a break in between for internships and work experiences to help better inform a student's interests? Should caregiving breaks become the norm in early career stages, and should the most productive working years begin after child-rearing?

Should new tax policies reward the period of caregiving years so that caregivers are not unduly penalized for financial security?

This opportunity requires innovators like you, the reader, to develop new ways to support a multistage life, most of which have yet to be recognized by society. There may be no retirement. There will be "unretirement." Twenty-year-olds and seventy-year-olds will be learning together remotely or in classrooms at universities around the world. We will see multiple sabbatical opportunities, transition planning companies, and new ways to support caregivers. New financial tools and policies will enable people to withdraw from their 401(k) accounts to support their continuous education, without penalty. There will be multigenerational customers who use products and services that can span fifty to sixty years.

To help consumers, marketers, and businesses address all these new needs and possibilities, we need a new framework for both recognizing the multistage life and naming the new stages. It is not just longer middle age. It is not extended seniorhood or elderhood. It is more than that. It is a reimagining of the life course that can span one hundred years.

The rest of this book is dedicated to helping you understand, adapt to, and seize on this demographic phenomenon. We start by recognizing that the most important thing about everyone living longer is not the number of years but the stages they'll go through—stages that no other people have experienced. And we'll start by examining and naming the new stages.

● RECOMMENDATIONS

- Change your mindset. The three-stage life is an anachronism. People will be living century-long lives.

- Know this statistic: by 2050, the number of people fifty and older is projected to double, and people aged sixty-five and older will outnumber children fifteen and younger for the first time in history worldwide.

- Remember that people fifty and over account for more than 50 percent of consumer spending in the United States and 83 percent of household wealth. This demographic represents the largest and one of the fastest-growing business opportunities in the United States and worldwide.

- Consider that this is not just an opportunity for the fifty-plus demographic. It also encompasses a much broader spectrum that includes intergenerational products and services for a century-plus life.

- Integrate the stage, not age, concept when thinking about the longevity opportunities. The new maps of life will have many new stages, will not be defined by age, and will produce a wealth of new opportunities.

- Aim for extending healthspan, not just lifespan.

- Factor stage and multigenerational perspectives into your strategy in product design, consumer services, and marketing strategies.

CHAPTER 2

Many Ages, Many Stages

With longer lifespans and healthspans, so-called old people can't be lumped together as one demographic. The vocabulary we use to describe older adults was based on age and is no longer accurate or relevant. Here, I develop a new vocabulary to frame an understanding of the diverse lives of older people. By resetting our language, we will understand the longevity market better and overcome persistent ageism traps.

Consider these three people:

Eduardo has just completed his tenth Grand Prix race in Monaco. He loves to race cars, rides an electric bicycle to work every day, and runs the business he started in his late twenties. He recently completed a year-long university program for professionals who want to recharge and become continuous learners. He skis each winter with his family and can only be described as thoroughly enjoying life and contributing to making his community a better place. Eduardo also enjoys traveling the world with his wife.

Maria has been a widow for ten years. She has several chronic conditions, including heart disease, diabetes, and pulmonary disease, and recently had a stroke. Her recovery took three months, and Medicare did not pay for nonskilled home care. Her daughter, Erin, an only child who lives across the country, took a unpaid leave of absence from her career at an investment firm to care for her mother's daily needs. Maria is now using this time with her daughter to discuss her wishes for future health care and her legacy.

Kim has just started a new company creating a line of clothing for older women who are active but do not fit into "younger" Lululemon-style products. She visits distributors around the country and conducts focus groups with women to learn about product improvements and new opportunities. She uses her own products in her dancing and exercise classes, which she loves to attend.

Now try to rank each person from youngest to oldest. You might suspect that Kim and Eduardo, who are active, are younger, while Maria, who has been ailing, is the oldest.

All three are seventy-five. But not all three are elderly or old. Can they all be called senior? Maybe, but that term does nothing to help describe the varied activities, needs, and desires of the three.

It is in fact absurd to group all these individuals together or to use the same words to classify them. Each person is experiencing the same lifespan but with a different healthspan. Eduardo has both a lifespan and a healthspan full of vigor and purpose. Maria has more serious medical issues and requires assistance and caregiving. She may sound more stereotypically old in her frailness and limited functionality. Even so, the word *old* inadequately captures Maria's stage and what it means to serve it. Kim is vibrant in her entrepreneur (olderpreneur) stage, actively building her business.

The words we typically use to describe people over sixty-five refer to age and are not only insufficient but also erroneous. The idea that a single term can encompass a thirty- to forty-year span of life simply doesn't work anymore. Not only is it reductive, but it simply isn't accurate. More than half of the people who reach eighty-five years will be in good health, and the same proportion of Americans surveyed expect to be working well beyond their seventies.[1] Words like *senior, silver,* and even *retiree* simply aren't right.

This may seem a small point, but the language we use shapes our understanding and beliefs. A more sophisticated understanding of this market demands a more sophisticated language to describe it. If we don't find the right words, we will marginalize a productive part of society while also missing the burgeoning opportunity to serve it.

So far, the language hasn't evolved enough. As I recounted in chapter 1, my friend Marc said that despite being seventy, he felt forty-five. He is an active lawyer, an accomplished musician, an investor, and a rock concert aficionado. He is also a caregiver for his father, who is in his nineties. Marc says he often feels dismissed as simply old, a description that runs counter to how he sees himself. "I am still able to accomplish what I want in life at this stage as I could three decades ago," he says. "I am, sadly, not perceived that way."

The new language must focus on the many stages people find themselves in, because it's likely that older adults who are the same age are part of completely different market segments. Many of the products and services that interest them will vary. After hearing a panel talk about the topic, one student who internalized this new mindset cleverly put it this way: *"If you've seen one seventy-five-year-old, you've seen one seventy-five-year-old."* Swap in any age you want, and the observation still applies.

Developing and then deploying a new language around stage and not age isn't easy. Marketers are trying, though, in part because older adults controlled more than $8.3 trillion of spending power in 2018, and this number will triple to $28.2 trillion by 2050.[2] So you'll see new catchwords coming out in the branding of companies already seizing the opportunity.

But getting it right isn't always easy. Take companies like Silver Bills and Silvernest. Silver Bills provides bill-paying services, and Silvernest helps empty nesters rent rooms to students and professionals. Both services are good ideas, but not everyone they're targeting (like Marc) identifies as *silver.* Moreover, some in this age range would actively avoid that association, because the term is keyed to age, that is, being old enough to have gray hair. Many people who could use these products may be in different stages and would require tweaks to the products themselves and to the communications they receive. But the companies haven't developed the language to describe the stages of people in this demographic.

Many other companies have glommed on to the word *third* as well, as in *third act* or *third stage*. Once again, phrases like these signify temporal marking and rather ominously imply it's the *last* act. As we'll see, when you view the world through stages, you can see many, many more acts.

How do we capture the mindset of going forward into new chapters of life, new stages, new purposes, and new adventures rather than ending them?

Don't Call Me Old

We shouldn't judge companies like Silver Bills and Silvernest too critically. It has proven difficult to create a new vernacular for this more nuanced view of the market. Debates continue about how best to develop this vocabulary and to whom it should apply. For example, in one poll, only 16 percent of adults sixty or older thought of sixty-five as old, while an overwhelming majority of people between eighteen and twenty-nine said it was.[3]

I have identified more than fifty labels being tried out as a way to describe the "new old age," including:

Explorers	Young old	Distinguished
Middlers	Yold	New age of aging
Middlescence	Better old age	Bloomers
Perennials	Legacy years	Experienced
Generation B	Elderhood	Wise ones
New old	Olderhood	Modern elders
New old age	Vintage	Pre-old

When you collect enough terms, you start to see categories like colors (gray, graying, silver, golden); flowers (perennials, bloomers); of course, the letters (Gen B for boomers, Generation R for retirees); and the made-up words ("middlers," "middlescence," "oldster," "olderhood," and the frankly weird-sounding "yold").

Few of these terms have captured the affection or the attention of those who receive those labels. None of these terms reflects the vitality and variability of this thirty-plus-year addition to lives. And none adequately reflects the new opportunities.

In early 2020, I launched the Naming Project as part of the Longevity Innovations Special Interest Group I lead at the Stanford Distinguished Careers Institute. The project brought together a diverse, multidisciplinary group of people to brainstorm ideas for how to name the new stages that longer lives create. We also brought in an expert instructor in design thinking from the Hasso Plattner Institute of Design at Stanford (d.school) to help guide this intergenerational project.

We interviewed people fifty to eighty-five years old and learned about their life journeys, experiences, and reactions to various labels often assigned to them. We also included the graduate students' perspectives on aging, whom they viewed as old or older, and the language they would like to see being used for these new stages when they arrive healthy and energetic in their sixties, seventies, and eighties.

In our project workshop, we framed the problem, came up with ideas for a new lexicon, and prototyped and pitched them. We learned that in other languages and cultures, the word for *older* implies earned wisdom and is revered. In our culture and language, *older* implies ending and declining. We aimed to capture the wisdom, the vibrancy, the experience, and the confidence that comes with these years.

Out of more than fifty terms circulating, we found that the most common and least offensive current term to describe the longevity customer was *older adult*. The term Gen B (originally coined by Arthur Bretschneider, CEO of Seniorly) was also inoffensive but was less applicable for future generations.[4] It would be confusing for, say, Gen Z to become Gen B later on.

Much of the discussion ended up centering on aging well, or successful and healthy aging. And of course, we agreed that the language should aim to describe stages, not ages. We also generally agreed that the words to describe the people in these new stages needed to reflect their vitality, and their roles as doers, actualizers, trailblazers, players, and leaders, to name just a few (figure 2-1).

In our workshop, teams pitched the names they felt they would be comfortable with being called. Four emerged that resonated with most attendees:

- Stagers

- Early bloomers and late bloomers

- Wellders

- ZoomRz

FIGURE 2-1

Some new terms describing the longevity customer

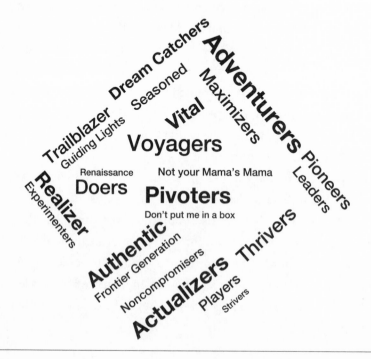

Different words will resonate with different people. For example, the term *renaissance years* resonates for me personally. A renaissance is "a renewal of life, vigor, interest, rebirth and revival." The goal here isn't to settle on a single term but rather to begin to change the language away from time-based words to stage-based ones.

I still ask friends and older adults what they want to be called. My friend Sam suggested the furthers, or the further-mores, which he says describes what he's doing as an avid cyclist and a frequent user of online classes: he's furthering his health and education. His ninety-five-year-old mother-in-law, Sylvia, swims every day at the local community pool and attends the Fromm Institute for Lifelong Learning. And while she is in poorer health than Sam is and needs some caregiving, Sylvia is as purposeful in her life as he is, despite their twenty-five-year age difference. Both are vibrant and looking forward and going further.

While the Naming Project is not quite done with exploring and testing out new names in different focus groups, the concept of using the right terminology will be important for you as an innovator, a marketer, or a CEO. More significantly, you will need to understand the new mindset of the longevity customer as you develop a marketing strategy for older adults (or older people). It is far more important to remember and understand stages than it is finding the perfect label. Market to older adults as if they have many of the attributes and attitudes of younger customers but may need slightly different product features. And, crucially, don't make the features that are geared toward their age the selling points. You sell to stage, not age. (All these features are discussed in detail in chapter 5.)

Defining the Stages

Besides naming the new overall period of life created by longevity, we also have a growing need to identify and name the phases and stages within this demographic. The classic three-stage life—learn, earn, retire—is no longer relevant. The language we need now must be more varied because of the many stages that are emerging, and it must be more flexible because stages no longer map to age in a clear or linear fashion.

For the rest of this book we'll use eighteen stages as our organizing principle. They are loosely grouped together in table 2-1.

I will discuss these stages in more depth in coming chapters. For now, note that not all the stages map to age neatly. People will find themselves in more than one stage at a time. The movement between stages will hardly be linear. Many people will likely have multiple career breaks to take care of children or older parents, for educational leaves, and for rejuvenation opportunities and sabbaticals. My friend Marc is both in the repurposing stage of his longevity years, as he explores and devotes time to his love of music, and in a caregiving stage, as he works to assist and enhance the later years of his ninety-five-year-old father. Maria, who has several serious illnesses, is nearing her legacy stage and possibly her end-of-life stage. After I took a break for a caregiving stage (which overlapped with my developing financial security stage), I am now in my renaissance and portfolio stages, discovering an array of new and interesting career opportunities and connecting with new communities of innovators, leaders, and those committed to having an impact.

TABLE 2-1

The eighteen stages of life

Growth stages	Career and family stages	Reinvention stages	Closing stages
Starting	Continuous learning	Repurposing	Legacy
Growing	Developing financial security	Relaunching	End of life
First launch		Resetting life priorities	
Experimenting	Parenting/family		
	Caregiving	Transition	
	Optimizing health	Portfolio	
		Renaissance	
		Sidepreneur	

Replacing the Idea of Retirement

You won't see the word *retirement* among the stages, for good reason. Much that is changing makes this stage less useful as an organizing principle. For one, the age of retirement is shifting upward. For another, the economic reality of living healthily into your eighties, nineties, or beyond means retirement may not be an easy option. Finally, there's the desire for healthy older adults to not *want* to retire. The notion that everyone over sixty-five is retirement age is an antiquated one.

Instead, within the old retirement stage, you'll now find multiple stages like these:

- Repurposing: moving a career focus to a new central purpose

- Relaunching: doing all the activities that allow you to start a new part of your life, like learning

- Transitioning: facilitating the move from one identity to another

- Resetting life priorities: recoding a value system to support new priorities and goals

A big part of what used to be retirement will now be learning. In fact, learning will span all parts of life in a more meaningful way instead of being that thing you did at the beginning. Both individuals and companies will increasingly need to integrate transition planning and upskilling throughout careers and over time. New businesses will continue to emerge to support these multiple life stages and transitions.

New Entrepreneurs

One surprising by-product of longer lives and the new business opportunities presented by longevity is a sharp increase in the number of successful businesses started by older adults. A sixty-year-old who launches a business is three times more likely to succeed than a thirty-year-old peer. More than 50 percent of the most successful startups are founded by people over fifty. A 2016 study of startup activity in the United States by the Ewing Marion Kaufmann Foundation revealed that 25 percent of new entrepreneurs are fifty-five to sixty-four.[5] In 2018, the US Census State of Small Business Survey revealed that there are more business owners aged fifty to fifty-nine than any other age group, with many using their wealth of career experience, professional contacts, and financial stability to build thriving companies.[6]

The earned experience that older adults often have along with their skills helps them succeed. Further, in addressing this market opportunity, these older people often have the valued perspective and insights of the market. Because they are living the stages that younger people may not yet have fully internalized, older adults better understand the needs and stages of the varied older adult consumer.

Due to growing recognition and momentum, incubators and accelerators have begun to increase in number in the United States and Canada to foster older entrepreneurs. And a variety of new terms are being floated to capture these trends (e.g., *olderpreneurs* and *seniorpreneurs*), but those tend to fall short as they are still focused on age, not stage. Contrast those terms with one I like: *sidepreneurs*, a term coined initially by American Express.[7] Sidepreneurs are defined as women business owners who work fewer than twenty hours per week on their businesses. Between 2014 and 2019, this group grew by 39 percent, partly a reflection of the sharing economy and partly due to increased longevity and the number of older adults entering a new stage. But notice how the term doesn't actually focus on age but implies a different life stage.

Suffice to say, this new crop of innovators and entrepreneurs has experience, purpose, and passion and will contribute greatly to business and society in the future.

The Five-Quarter Life

The terms for stages and their definitions are still evolving—there are any number of efforts underway—and the lexicon can get confusing. For our purposes, we need one framework that we can apply throughout the rest of this book to capture the many stages and how they may play out over a lifetime.

As mentioned earlier, we'll use a framework I call the five quarters, or 5Qs. Yes, I know that's funky math, but the idea is to capture the notion of extra time that was once unavailable to us but that is now available because of our increased longevity and healthspan.

The 5Qs are an umbrella that can capture the range of stages that individuals will go through in a hundred-year life. But again, this doesn't mean that one stage can only exist in one quarter.

People may generally be labeled under this framework as stagers or perhaps one of the other new phrases suggested by our Naming Project. For now, I am using the coined term *furtherhood* to represent the new stages of longevity that can occur for people in the third through fifth parts of their lives (Q3–Q5), as outlined below. Furtherhood can occur anytime for people who are over sixty and have much to look forward to.

Here are the five quarters (see also figure 2-2):

- Q1, the Starting Quarter: This quarter encompasses ages traditionally from birth to thirty years. In this quarter, people are starting to talk, walk, and learn. They are starting new chapters in high school, college, or work. They may be starting families; this quarter could extend into people's thirties.

- Q2, the Growing Quarter: The growing quarter is roughly when individuals are building their adult lives filled with work

FIGURE 2-2

The five-quarter (5Q) life framework

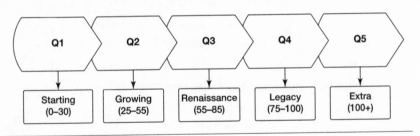

and career explorations, transitions, career breaks, and continuous learning. Q2 is likely to occur between ages twenty-five and fifty-five. People here are growing their lives and maybe building their family, their community, their relationships, and their finances. They are often reexamining each of these components of life throughout this quarter. Q2 may also be characterized by upskilling, continuous learning, and components of Q3 in anticipation of long-lived lives and work. This quarter often includes significant caregiving for children or parents, and often for both.

- **Q3, the Renaissance Quarter:** This is a time of *re*'s: repurposing, rejuvenation, renaissance, and reevaluation. Q3 could be called the re-everything. It is filled with continuous learning and exploration and is perhaps more of a portfolio lifestyle. This quarter may occur sometime between ages fifty and eighty-five. For some people, Q3 may well last into their mid-eighties and conceivably their nineties. In Q3, individuals may indeed start new careers or return to school for more education and upskilling. They may start new families, continue to care for children or parents, or become involved in caregiving for their grandchildren. Work may be just one of many priorities in this quarter. Often, this quarter may become what have been called the *portfolio years*—the period when people engage in a range of purposeful activities, only some of which are paid. These years may offer a vibrant entrepreneurial opportunity and may include mentoring, advising, and investing.

- **Q4, the Legacy Years:** As individuals enter their fourth quarter, they may reassess their healthspan, which will determine what types of activities and stages they can engage in. For many people, Q4 may last well into their eighties and beyond. Q4 will invariably involve more concerns about changing medical needs and support. However, it can also be filled with new opportunities to define one's legacy.

FIGURE 2-3

Example of an individual's 5Q life

An example of how longevity stages span many ages. Imagine Maria lived to 100. Here are some of the stages she would experience across her five-quarter life. Note how some stages continue through multiple ages and others repeat at different times. Also note that Maria was a longevity customer well before she turned 60, as a caregiver in Q2.

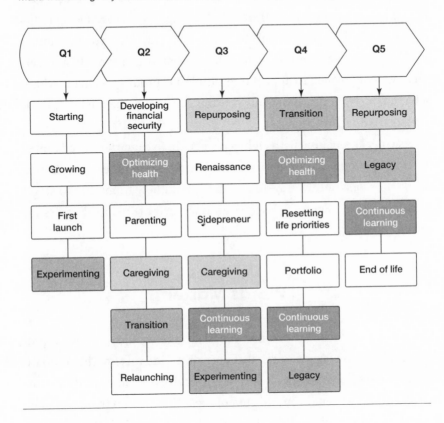

- Q5, the Extra Years: The fifth quarter is bonus time that may or may not come with increased healthspan and may not have been anticipated. Most people are generally expected to need some form of assistance in the last five years of life. Since babies born today should expect to live into their hundreds, how you use those years of added longevity will largely depend on how well you invested in and maintained your healthspan and financial security.

At the beginning of this chapter, you met Eduardo, Maria, and Kim, all of whom are seventy-five. (Go back and reread those descriptions if you want.) Eduardo and Kim are in Q3; Maria is in Q4. In using this paradigm, we must recognize that within each quarter, multiple stages of life can be occurring, such as those just described. You might be a caregiver, for example, in Q1 or Q4. You might need caretaking in Q4 or not at all. This insight will help you recognize that your customer and end user may well be different and that your products and services will often need to appeal to multiple age groups and generations. Chapter 5 elaborates more on who the consumer, the payer, and the end user are.

As you can imagine with eighteen stages in five quarters, the number of combinations is countless, but we can cross-map these two frameworks to scope out lives and help understand how to market to stages within quarters. Figure 2-3 shows an imagined life mapped across the two frameworks.

Words Matter

One of the reasons we need new language and should shift our mindset from age to stage is to combat ageism. In identifying the new language to describe the new stages of longer lives, we need to defy some of the existing prejudices and stereotypes. Not only do these biases do an injustice to older adults, but frankly, these prejudices also cause companies and investors to miss massive opportunities from a diverse, thriving population prepared to contribute to society more than people expect.

At the core of ageism is a stereotypical assumption that when people turn sixty-five, they become dependent on others for financial assistance and direct care, grow frail and sickly, and end up in residential care.[8]

Ageism may be directed toward older people by younger generations or may be internalized by someone as a sense of diminished value as they age.[9] Ageism can take many forms in work environments and is influenced by how companies think of their customers. In many tech firms in Silicon Valley, a forty-year-old can feel old, obsolete even.

Ageism and age diversity have been touchy issues, and companies and other organizations are increasingly identifying ways to approach them. Surveys conducted by Transamerica Institute in 2017 show that for younger people, the word *old* tends to be a number somewhere around sixty—much lower than what older generations consider old.[10] This finding may seem somewhat unsurprising but is nevertheless important to understand, given the threat of ageism in an aging workforce, Transamerica warns.

Starting with language, which shapes how we think about older people, ageism's effects are pernicious. Ageism affects women most significantly in the workplace, as they often need to take career breaks for caregiving, before returning to the workforce at a later stage or age. Increasingly, men are taking career breaks and want to participate in the workforce without fear of ageism impacting their roles and opportunities. Indeed, considering people's longevity and the growing shortage of caregivers, most workers will need to take one or more career breaks along their work-life journey.

The new longevity requires a new mindset that eliminates ageism both in the workplace culture and in the development and marketing of new products and services to address the longevity market. And this new mindset starts with the words we use.

What Does Resetting the Conversation Mean to My Business?

These new paradigms may help you better understand both your customer and your employee. Imagine the difference between selling a new car to a "senior" by offering new, larger dials and easier entry and selling a new car to a "renaissance adult" who is eager to have a new car with better features, all of which are stealth. (By stealth, I mean a product that addresses specific needs of older customers with features designed for an older adult's needs but that doesn't specifically call them out, e.g., larger dials or color contrasts. More on this in chapter 5.) Also think of the end user of your products and services over the life course. Ideally, you want to develop products and services that can serve multiple generations so that younger and older customers may enjoy the stealth features you may build into your prototypes.

Consider the increased productivity you will gain from your employees if you better understand what stage (not age) they are at, so that your employment policies could be better adapted to their needs. They may want to continue to work but no longer need child care benefits. Or they may need caregiving benefits for older parents, regardless of their age.

Ageism also affects the negative way the longevity customer may be viewed, complete with stereotypes about capabilities, needs, and wants. Without the benefit of an intergenerational workforce, product development could be limited by ageist views of the longevity customer. Addressing ageism can benefit your company's culture, your employees' health costs, and, most significantly, your firm's ability to better understand the needs and wants of the longevity customer.

Marketing to this customer will require new strategies and new considerations. Understanding the multiple-stage life course will enhance your ability to do so effectively. Chapter 3 provides a framework on how to view the new longevity customer.

RECOMMENDATIONS

- Use the right terminology for older consumers and customers. It will be important for you as an innovator, a marketer, or a leader of a company.

- Remember that people will in fact be younger for longer and will prioritize different stages at different times in their life course.

- Think of older adults in their renaissance years, as opposed to their end-of-life years.

- Create an intergenerational workforce. It will benefit your product development and market success and will help eliminate ageist views of the longevity customer.

- Eliminating ageism in your organization, has many benefits: improved company culture, reduced employee health costs, and, most significantly, smarter marketing and your firm's ability to better understand the needs and wants of the longevity customer.

CHAPTER 3

Marketing to Stage

We cannot segment the longevity market by creating age ranges within the extra thirty to forty years of life that the demographic now includes. Instead, we need multiple lenses to create three segmentations: demographic, domain, and stage. Combined, these three ways of looking at the longevity market will help you understand it and how it differs from traditional markets. For example, the multiple-lens view will help you understand how purchases are made, when the user and the purchaser are different people, who the decision maker is, and how you should communicate product features. By using the three segments, you'll gain the nuance you need to successfully serve the longevity market.

The new lifespan and healthspan create various more nuanced life progressions. Think of a growing tree. A three-foot-high tree's branches expand in a few directions. You may see, say, four limbs, each limb with three branches and a few twigs per branch. A thirty-foot tree, on the other hand, expands into dozens of limbs with hundreds of branches and thousands of twigs holding leaves. The extension of life and good health by decades creates a similar exponential effect on life experiences.

Anything this complex needs organizing principles. In a tree, we use some of the terms I just used to segment it: limbs, branches, twigs, leaves. We use other ideas—new growth, old growth, flowering, and so forth—to understand the complex system too.

In the longevity market, we need similarly robust segmentation. In this chapter, we'll explore some of the efforts at that and how they'll help you understand and serve the market.

Those that do recognize the opportunity have started to think about more than just trees and are creating sophisticated segmentation efforts. In the past five years, I've found no fewer than ten different efforts at segmenting the longevity market into dozens of domains. More are added each year, and platforms that provide information across many segments are emerging.[1]

Unfortunately, many businesses don't segment this market at all. The average person doesn't even know about the demographic shift taking place, and the average business is only slightly more aware. To keep with the metaphor, most businesses don't see leaves and twigs and branches, they just see a tree. They pick an age, say, sixty, and everyone over that age is the segment. And that's if they consider the segment in their strategies at all.

Many great ideas for serving this market have failed because they approached the market with age-only segmentation—companies decide they'll serve the "silver" or "gray" market and create products for "old" people. But that's just one limb on a really big tree.

We'll take a more sophisticated approach by sorting the market and its customers into three segments that are helpful to group and describe the many sorts of customers in the longevity market:

- Demographics

- Domain

- Stage

The real magic happens when you understand each segment and its nuances and then map stages onto them. Let's take each in turn.

Demographic Segmentation

Attributes: Age, Functionality and Health, Education,
Income, Geography, Ethnicity, Attitude

The most obvious attribute of demographics here, age, is also the most misleading one for the longevity customer. It's a mistake to consider all needs similar and to try to capture them in a this-age-or-older market. For the longevity customer, the single most important indicator in demographic segmentation is health status and functional health. Of course, the greatest influencer on health status is education.

Age

In a society where living to one hundred is the norm, companies should avoid categorizing buying patterns, motivation, lifestyles, and needs as homogenous and based primarily on age. Stage is important to combine with age in demographics segmentation.

Some marketers have crept into this idea by incorporating into their plans gerontology experts' descriptions of aging.[2] These descriptions hint at, but don't quite capture, true stages:

- New old or young old: 65–74

- Old or middle old: 75–84

- Old-old: 85+

This delineation is based on broad data that suggests some linear relationship between age and functionality or overall health. But those relationships are getting more complicated with increased healthspan. If these categories are meant to suggest overall health, they simply don't work anymore. There are old-old seventy-two-year-olds and new old seventy-five-year-olds. More than half of people over eighty-five feel they can still work, which hardly sounds old-old.

Functionality and Health

Another way to fine-tune demographic segmentation is to add a layer of understanding where someone may be in their healthspan. The Gerontological Society of America has developed a helpful five-phase approach to describing functionality and health:[3]

- Go-go: excellent health, active, few or no limitations

- Go-slow: very good health, some self-limiting situations

- Slow-go: good health; needs assistance with activities of daily living

- Slow-slow: fair health; limitations on their activities of daily living

- No-go: physical and mental conditions that require the advanced care in senior nursing or assisted living facilities[4]

Such a paradigm is often used by financial services firms and advisers that segment their client's financial portfolio needs according to the person's activity levels, determined largely by healthspan. You may hear these terms, which can be helpful as a broad segmentation approach, but they are not as comprehensive when you are factoring in the longevity lens. There are vast differences in health and functionality among people sixty and older, and more than 50 percent of this group rate their health as good, and 25 percent rate it as excellent.

Education

Knowing a cohort's education level unlocks much information about that group; longevity customers are no exception. By far, the greatest predictor of successful aging is education. Healthspan and education are correlated, and education is, of course, closely correlated with income and wealth, which in turn will influence purchasing power.

The relationship between education and healthspan can become a virtuous cycle, too. The new healthspan unlocks opportunities for longevity customers in various stages to seek out more education, which in turn contributes to their good health and increased wealth. Whereas the education stage used to be largely limited to early life (school), then extended into professional life (continuing or adult education), you should now expect education to become a lifelong pursuit with massive opportunities in the longevity market.

Attitude

Marketers can also look at shifts that occur in older adults' outlook on life, independent of chronological age. It turns out that aging is something that everyone thinks about. Data shows that people in their twenties fear death the most, those in their thirties think about aging the most, while people in their seventies actually worry about aging the least.[5] Yet marketers traditionally focus on the effects of aging when communicating with longevity customers. Instead of age ranges, one report outlined five attitudes toward aging that marketers should focus on:

- Ageless adventurers: a journey of limitless opportunities and personal growth

- Communal caretakers: a time of engaging with community and enriching personal relationships

- Actualizing adults: a process of maturity and acquisition of adult responsibilities

- Future fearers: a time of anxiety and uncertainty due to risks associated with old age

- Youth chasers: a decline and loss of youth and vitality[6]

Notably, no numerical ages are associated with these attitudes. As described in chapter 2, Eduardo could be labeled an ageless adventurer, Kim an actualizing adult, and Maria a future fearer.

So when marketing to different types of older adults, images matter. Ageism matters. The people and images of older adults you portray should reflect adventurers as well as doers and not just the frail elder.

Wealth

All the preceding demographic segments affect wealth, and wealth will affect them as well. More than 53 percent of consumer-generated spending stems from the fifty-plus cohort. Yet, nearly half of older adults would be living in poverty without social security. This is an important dichotomy to understand about the longevity customer and the market composition. Designing products and services for affordability will be another important layer to your strategy and understanding.

• • •

Now we're starting to build something more than just a sixty-to-seventy-year-old segment. You may now be thinking about, say, a go-go (functionality and health) seventy-year-old (age) who takes online classes (education) and is becoming a grandparent (life events) and comfortable in their age (actualized adult).

Still there's more segmentation we can do.

Domain Segmentation

Understanding the customer demographics in more detail is a good start and should give you an appreciation of the amazing diversity in a group whose members are often lumped together as one thing, sixty-plus. Next, though, marketers need to consider the domains that have longevity opportunities and segment those out.

In short, opportunities are available in nearly every consumer-facing domain you can think of. Of course, there's health and wellness. But education as lifelong learning also becomes truly lifelong (sometimes referred to as long-life learning). Work is another relevant domain, as more people work into their seventh and eighth decades. Naturally, finance through saving and investing for a longer life is a massive domain. Food and nutrition opportunities abound as well. Housing is another domain that can cater to the longevity market. And then there's leisure, travel, entertainment, fashion. It's hard to imagine a domain without a gaping hole ready to be filled by companies that want to invest in the longevity opportunity and the many stages older adults will find themselves in.

More domains are being identified each year, as new technologies emerge to offer new ways to enhance a multistage life course. Within those domains are many subdomains. For example, in the caregiving domain, new products and services are exploding. The domain has subdomains focused on the caregiver, the recipient, and the health-care professional, all of whom are involved in caregiving transactions. Telehealth products, for example, may focus on new longevity-tuned UX for the care recipient or on secure transactions for the medical professional. It may be the hardware supplied to the patient or the software used by the caregiver. More suggested subdomains and solutions are detailed in chapter 4.

Many groups have tried to formalize the domains. One effort that I've found useful breaks the domains into eight life-stage priorities and eleven service areas (table 3-1).[7]

You may not have thought of fashion and accessories as a longevity domain. Then again, Kim from the last chapter found an opportunity in fitness clothing for active older adults. Similarly, travel and entertainment will increasingly be redesigned to accommodate the wants and needs of the longevity consumer, such as Eduardo and his family. And most innovators and entrepreneurs have not yet understood the importance of creating digital literacy for successful aging and for the education and training market, which would have benefited Maria, who is in poor health.

A networking organization called Aging2.0 offers another example. Its platform, the Collective, is building global innovation collaborative groups in eight areas, called grand challenges.[8] Think of these as domains and the areas of focus as possible subdomains:

- Engagement and purpose: Helping older adults get and stay meaningfully engaged is critical for their health and the health of our communities. Among the areas of focus here are the digital

TABLE 3-1

Key domains to target in the longevity market

Life-stage priorities	Service and product realms
Home and housing	Housing and home modification
Money and security	Financial services
Health and longevity	Transportation
Caregiving and family	Health care
Purpose and giving	Food and nutrition
Spirituality and identity	Personal care
Learning and connection	Long-term and memory care
Civic life and community	Fashion and accessories
	Wellness
	Training and education
	Travel, media, and entertainment

Source: Adapted from Susan Conley, "Longevity Market Map," Stria News, 2019.

divide, social inclusion, lifelong learning, encore careers, disrupting retirement, volunteering, meaning, and legacy.

- **Financial wellness:** Traditional models of work and retirement have not kept pace. To finance this increasing longevity, areas of focus include later-life employment; new models for planning for, and financing, care; and scams and fraud prevention.

- **Mobility and movement:** Everyday objects, homes, and communities are not originally designed with longevity in mind. They often become obstacles to movement, safety, independence, and socializing. Areas of focus include safety, strength, balance, fitness, independence, and mobility.

- **Daily living and lifestyle:** Two-thirds of people over sixty-five need no assistance with daily living. Products and services for those who do need assistance are common, but new areas of focus can serve those who don't. These new areas include lifestyle, passion projects, active-lifestyle hobbies, and travel.

- **Caregiving:** Caregiving is a combination of formal and informal services, professional and family-based. With longer lives may come more caregiving. Family caregivers often juggle other family and work responsibilities while living remotely from the care recipient. Areas of focus here can help those caregivers and include support, training, resources, and tools to effectively provide care.

- **Care coordination:** Desire to care for people in the least restrictive, most cost-effective setting possible is a goal. Areas of focus include new tools and new models to support care transitions, clinical collaboration, medication management, population health management, and remote care delivery.

- **Brain health:** Maximizing cognitive ability and brain health is a priority for aging societies as the number of people with cognitive limitations and mental health issues continues to rise. A focus on new approaches, tools, and services to enhance treatment and to support caregivers is crucial.

- **End of life:** Too often the way people experience the end of life fails to honor how they have lived their lives. The focus here is on emergent technologies and collaborative efforts to create dignified and positive end-of-life experiences.

These are just a few of the new market opportunities being identified from the longevity lens, which will be further examined in chapter 4.

A useful exercise for leaders is to think about domains and subdomains in terms of their own strategy. In which of these areas could you find new opportunities? Are there other subdomains you can imagine for longevity customers?

Stage Segmentation

All these lenses are valuable from a product development or business ideation standpoint. You can use these paradigms in combination to segment the market you are targeting, to help develop your product or service prototype, and to develop a comprehensive marketing strategy. But another segmentation is needed to integrate the broader needs that hundred-year lives, truly multistage lives, will require.

It is stage, not age, that, above all, should drive segmentation efforts. Beyond demographics and the domain you're in, ask yourself, Is my customer in the launching stage of their life course or in the repurposing stage? You could have two customers in repurposing, one in their forties, and one in their seventies. Understanding your customers' different stages will help you create products that fit your market and help you tailor your marketing strategies accordingly. Increasingly, you will adopt the attitude that you are aiming for a multigenerational customer base and that one product or service may serve many demographics.

I've outlined the eighteen stages in chapter 2 and how they fit into the 5Q framework. Combining those stages with demographics and domains creates the smartest, most sophisticated segmentation for the longevity market. It will show how marketing strategies will differ *within* the longevity market in light of this more complete picture.

For example, as described earlier, Eduardo, Maria, and Kim are all seventy-five. All are at different stages, with varied demographic profiles despite their similar age, and appealing as customers to different domains.

Eduardo

Eduardo has already reserved a place in a local retirement community, should he and his wife need one in the future. From his perspective, this move is likely to happen a decade or more in the future, maybe when they're in their nineties. Eduardo does not like to use any social media. Marketing to him as a senior, a silver, or an elderly person would be a huge mistake. He doesn't consider himself old. Calling out the features of products or services tailored to someone his age will only remind him of his demographic status. You can provide these features but should not highlight them. He is eager to continue traveling and seeking adventure with his family, including his children and grandchildren.

Two of Eduardo's stages are continuous learner and renaissance. Marketing to those stages and not to Eduardo's seventy-five years means he would be a great target for, say, intergenerational travel and learning experiences for him and his family or younger friends he has made in his recent classes. He may also need new accessories for his bicycle to enhance his visual field while riding. Most bicycle makers have yet to create the accessories or design for older bike riders. They may find inspiration from Nike's experience developing a new type of athletic shoe for older athletes (see chapter 4). However, Eduardo does have mild hearing loss, so products and services that would enhance his enjoyment of concerts, other performances, and dinner conversation in restaurants would be highly desirable as long as they're not marketed as products for seniors.

Marketing to Eduardo and his wife would be best viewed as marketing to an active adult and a lifelong learner, and that's it. Even if the features you develop for Eduardo are tailored to someone his age, that's not the value to him as someone in good health and in a renaissance.

By the way, in the United States, there are about sixteen million Eduardos, and the number is growing.

Maria

Maria is in ill health, and her thirty-six-year-old daughter, Erin, has invested much money in traveling to see her mother and take care of her. Erin justified spending the money to travel because "if this was the last time we could be together, I should be there." Erin is unaware that although Maria's health is not good, she may live many more years. And the money Erin has spent as a caregiver could have been invested in professional caregiving that may have better helped her mother.

Maria is probably in a legacy stage, but what you should be thinking about here are Erin's stages: caregiving, parenting, developing financial security. Marketing to Maria would be a missed opportunity. It is her daughter who should be the target of the many products and services that could have been used to support Maria. Yet, because Erin is in her thirties, none of these products and services have been routinely marketed to her or her demographic. She is not the age, yet she is integrally involved in the caregiving stage. Had companies thought to find the *daughter/decision maker/influencer* role through her networks on social media, they would have approached marketing where she interacts with products and services.

Specifically, a geriatric care manager service could help Maria's daughter. Erin has never heard of this kind of service. A new initiative, Daughterhood, has recognized the importance and role of the daughter or daughter-in-law in both caring for older people and acting as decision maker or chief purchasing officer. Daughterhood has created a platform where needs, products, and services are shared across the country, so that daughters—and, increasingly, sons—have access to better information about how to care for their parents and loved ones. New companies are emerging to offer concierge-type services for this market. The concierge serves as a navigator for families and individuals, offering a rage of nonmedical care management for the older family member and transitional services when this person is discharged from the hospital.

Maria's situation and that of her daughter, Erin, are among the most common in the United States. Women live longer than men do and are widowed sooner, and a third of women live alone. Their children frequently need either to provide care while continuing to work or to make financial sacrifices during that period. Financial services for people in their thirties, then, is a longevity market opportunity. Erin will most likely be the purchaser of any extra services for her mother, including a geriatric care manager or a concierge, if only someone would market these services to her.

Kim

Although Kim has just started her new company, she sometimes feels alone with all the decisions an entrepreneur must make. She could benefit from new coworking spaces for older entrepreneurs (these facilities were just emerging before the Covid-19 pandemic, and some have gone virtual for the time being). Incubators for olderpreneurs are also becoming more common. Kim is in the sidepreneur and experimenting stages and perhaps the repurposing stage as she reenters work after taking a break as a caregiver. She also needs to learn new tech skills that have been developed during her career break. Soon she may discover she's in the continuous learner stage as well. Companies focusing on digital literacy would benefit Kim. She is in a dynamic position with many needs from many stages. And there are many people like Kim—more than 50 percent of the most successful startups are founded by people over fifty. And adults fifty-five and older are the fastest-growing segment of the workforce.[9]

Now you're seeing the power of segmentation that takes into account all these factors, and especially stage. Let's add one more example for good measure, this one from another seventy-five-year-old, Karim.

Karim

Karim is from France. He began smoking at age sixteen and immigrated to the United States at thirty-five. He worked for a long time as a waiter in a restaurant. He never married and has no children to care for him should he become ill or have diminished capacity. Karim has arthritis, and his mobility has declined. He wonders if he should move into a retirement community and worries whether he could actually afford one. He stays home most days, watches a lot of television, reads the newspapers, and misses the interaction of the customers and employees from the small restaurant he had worked in for thirty years. He is lonely. He sometimes wonders if he should move back to France to live with extended family.

Karim could be described as in the transition stage, and perhaps he's verging on the legacy stage. He will need a variety of services and products, most importantly to reduce his isolation. His primary sources of interaction are his doctors and his television. He needs a community, which in turn will open him up to new information and opportunities to make a transition and, hopefully, to enter a repurposing stage. New companies are targeting people like Karim with services to pick him up and bring him to social events, exercise classes, or other situations where he'll make new friends in the community.

Interestingly, as much as the companies offer these services to Karim, they are also marketing to insurers offering Medicare Advantage plans. For this reason, the payer of the service is not the end user. This arrangement creates major implications for the companies' strategy.

There are many Karims to serve, and serving them has cascading effects. Social isolation is one of the driving forces of medical costs in aging populations. Products and services that address social isolation help people and drive down costs.

What Does Marketing to Stage Mean for My Business?

As you can see, these domains represent massive markets, with at least ten thousand new customers on the horizon every day in the United States alone. From a stage standpoint, these markets encompass every family, every individual, and every business in century-long lives. This isn't just a health and wellness market opportunity. A host of industries will have new opportunities to innovate to address this growing demographic. Lifelong learning will become a new industry, for example. As people live longer, the traditional approach to education and work will change. A longer-living workforce will need to reskill for second, third, and fourth careers. Subscription models to education may become a new marketing strategy for these types of products and services. All these models will now also be affected by the realities of living in pandemic times.

Entertainment, travel, and media will all have a growing customer base. I recently spoke with a concert violinist who told me their orchestra was initially lamenting the declining attendance by young people. Then the musician realized that the client base was in fact growing with extended lifespans and healthspans, and the older concertgoer would be attending for much longer. They—older adults experiencing longer lives—were clearly the longevity opportunity for symphony and performance organizations. Covid-19 accelerated the development of digital memberships to events, museums, and more, and there will be a future for new virtual entertainment, learning, and travel.

Marketing to the longevity customer—who may not even be in the older adult demographic—will succeed best when stages are understood and when those stages are combined with a better demographic understanding, and a clear notion of the domains and subdomains companies want to work in.

One of the students who participated in a longevity course I've taught at the Stanford Graduate School of Business put it best: "I'm learning that care for the frail elderly is just a sliver of what longevity is about. My generation is going to live longer than anyone before us and the big question is: How do we adapt throughout our lives instead of sticking with antiquated systems, like retirement at sixty-five?"[10]

That student is right. There is an abundance of market opportunities and a range of longevity customers well beyond what you might imagine. It's time to delve deeper into some of those opportunities.

● RECOMMENDATIONS

- Use stage, not just age, to understand and segment your customer's needs and to decide how best to market to them.

- Do not uniformly lump customers into one age bracket, for example, people over fifty, sixty-five, or seventy. Instead, recognize the varied stages of life that individuals who will live to one hundred will embrace.

- Remember that hundred-year lives may encompass as many as eighteen different life stages and that most of these stages will occur independent of strict age guidelines and brackets. Longer lives will now entail a multistage and new phases approach, as outlined in chapter 2. It can help you profile and better understand your customer.

- Adopt the attitude that you are aiming for a multigenerational customer base. Companies will now need to consider developing products and services that simultaneously appeal to both younger and older consumers, as well as over many new life stages.

PART TWO

OPPORTUNITIES AND CHALLENGES

CHAPTER 4

Finding Your Longevity Opportunity

The longevity market will touch virtually every domain of products and services, including education, fintech, fashion and clothing, food and nutrition, leisure, travel, entertainment, housing, caregiving, and much more. These are all enormous markets, each with many subdomains. More product domains and subdomains are being identified each year with the emergence of such new technologies and innovations as intergenerational housing, digital literacy, and telehealth. Every company will need to develop a strategy based on domains and subdomains to address the new and growing market opportunities.

Recently, at one of the largest annual health-care conferences, a financial services company held a reception for women in health care. More than two hundred executive women from venture capital, banking, and wealth management attended. The firm was known for creating opportunities for women, including a returnship program to support women who take career breaks. The CEO, one of the most outstanding and respected leaders in finance and by any measure, was asked, "Women leaders here this evening, as well as your employees and many of your clients, will increasingly be living hundred-plus-year lives. This impacts women in unique ways. What is the longevity strategy for your company?" The CEO paused and then said, "We don't have one. That's a very good question."

If a plugged-in, widely respected leader who has already done so much for women in his organization and industry hasn't developed a longevity strategy, this suggests that others who aren't as progressive probably haven't, either. But such a strategy is imperative. Whether it's a strategy for your company or for starting a company, inaction isn't an option. A company's products, services, and workforce must all incorporate the new longevity and the many stages of longer lives.

There are two key strategies for this market: the expansion of a *corporate strategy*—in which a company adds this market to its portfolio of products and services—and the *entrepreneurial strategy*, in which you launch a venture to serve some domain within this market.

Segmentations, domains, and subdomains from chapter 2 will dictate how you shape your longevity strategy. Each presents its own challenges and potential solutions. For example, if you are trying to address the financial planning needs associated with longevity, that is the larger domain you are focused on, with many customers in multiple stages. Will you serve people in the end-of-life stage or people in a repurposing stage? Are your customers healthy and active? Considering the wide variation of customer attributes in this domain, you might struggle to develop products or services for such a broad population.

However, your strategy and the products that result may be clearer if you start with one segment and one stage, say, women in the renaissance stage. You know demographically that, compared with men, women live longer, on average earn less, and tend to be more risk-averse in their investment approach. You also know that in their renaissance stage, women are focused on investing in new passions and pursuits. Narrowing your focus is a smarter way to build a strategy.

As we explore different domains and subdomains for a longevity strategy, keep in mind that even the well-defined customer is complex. The person buying and paying may be a different person than the one the product is for. In this way, the longevity market mirrors products aimed at children but marketed to their parents.

Best practices for developing longevity strategies are already forming, and I'll provide case studies to show them. We will look at best practices in four areas:

- Identifying the strategy: redefining a business strategy to encompass the longevity market using a stage and not an age lens

- New and nontraditional strategies: defining a new strategy to meet emerging needs that grow out of the desire of older adults to age in place

- The care economy: defining and exploring the immense, complex, and growing caregiving market

- Emerging opportunities and nonobvious markets: defining new markets and workforce strategy opportunities that longer lives present and that may not be obvious

As we explore case studies of companies in these four areas, we'll identify the domain, subdomain, and stages being targeted, as identified in the previous chapter. We'll also look at these companies' best practices, which are instructive as you consider new longevity opportunities. One caveat: by the time this book goes to print, there may be several changes to the profiles of the companies highlighted. This is a growing and dynamic market; we will continue to see many mergers and acquisitions. There will be pivots and new customer acquisition strategies. Still, these cases are already a good framework for understanding the longevity market and how to get into it.

Identifying a Longevity Strategy

Companies that don't have a longevity strategy may be surprised to discover just how many opportunities there are and how lucrative they appear. Business leaders may wonder why they didn't think about a longevity strategy sooner. They'll also discover an active and constantly changing longevity market. Even while I was writing this book, there have been several major changes to the case studies I've examined and countless new entries vying for a piece of the market and serving different needs.

Profiled here are three companies and their approaches to identifying a longevity strategy: Merrill Lynch, Nike, and Warby Parker.

How Merrill Lynch Is Planning for Its Clients to Live to One Hundred

The financial services industry has been one of the first to recognize the longevity opportunity, as it sees its customers living longer and needing more money to sustain themselves over those extra years. Sadly and significantly, more than half of people over fifty say they don't have sufficient funds to support their retirement. This lack of financial security is a national concern and will require a significant call to action to avoid a disastrous financial downturn. As customers and clients prepare for longer lives, a variety of priorities and financial needs become powerful growth drivers.

Fidelity, Merrill Lynch, and Prudential have made significant investments in understanding the opportunity and challenges presented by a longer-living population. Merrill was one of the first to integrate longevity as part of its business strategy and its talent strategy, creating employee benefits that will help them in their own longevity.

Instead of being concerned that their clients were aging, Merrill Lynch reoriented the company around longevity as a core aspect of its business. The new focus makes sense: more than 80 percent of wealth was controlled by people sixty-five and older.[1]

The company began by developing its 7 Life Priorities program, which enhances retirement planning well beyond simple financial health to encompass finances, home, health, family, leisure, giving, and work.[2] Clients enrolled in the program don't just access their portfolio and get advice about what to do with their money. Assessment tools help them assign priority to which of the seven areas they're concerned with at their stage of life. This prioritization is then used to manage and periodically reassess portfolios.

In this case, Merrill is asking its clients to inform the company about what stage they might be in—even if the clients aren't thinking that way. A good way to get into this market is to survey your customers to see which stages seem most prevalent and might be worth targeting.

Merrill also helped its frontline staff understand their clients by hiring the financial industry's first gerontologist, in 2014. Advice is only as good as the adviser's ability to understand the stages, so the gerontologist provides training, education, and resources to engage clients on the topics of life planning, longevity, aging, and retirement to Merrill Lynch's fourteen thousand financial advisers. A big focus of this training is to shift the financial planners' focus so they don't base their advice on the client's age, for example, "People over eighty should do this." Now, stage is a crucial part of the financial planning.

Merrill Lynch created its own six major life stages for its clients and a map for understanding the needs within each stage as a way to help advisers set financial priorities. The six stages are early adulthood, parenting, caregiving, retirement, widowhood, end of life/legacy. Each of the six life stages has its own unique journey according to Merrill Lynch and is filled with key moments and financial considerations.

The company's integration of life priorities and stages enabled it to create more specific financial planning tools and products. What's more, Merrill Lynch turned its new strategy on itself, using the same framework for its employees. It did this by assessing employees' careers and people's desire for more time flexibility, caregiving support groups, and opportunities to work into retirement years. In 2021, the company introduced a variety of new elder-care benefits for its employees. Among these benefits are services to help coordinate elder care for family members and paid family leave for caregiving for older family members in their legacy and end-of-life stages.

Company: Bank of America Merrill Lynch

Domain: financial services

Subdomains: women investors and financial literacy; prevention of financial exploitation and elder abuse

Opportunity: $7–$8 trillion

Stages addressed: first launch through end of life—all eighteen stages ´

Best practices: hired a financial gerontologist to help design new products; introduced training for employees and clients; leadership publicly supported effort; offers elder-care benefits to employees

Merrill Lynch's model can be helpful, but it does not entirely reflect the stages we will use here and it is less detailed than our map of stages. Eduardo and Kim from chapter 2 are neither retired nor widowed. Maria's daughter, however, is a caregiver and is in early adulthood. Eduardo probably doesn't fit any of Merrill's stages. However, Merrill's combined approach could capture the financial needs of Eduardo, Kim, and Maria's daughter as they consider both their life priority and their financial stage.

The financial services industry has been one of the first to integrate stage rather than age into its marketing and product development strategy. Financial companies also understood the different subdomains of their industry. In a recent survey of financial advisers, 29 percent identified longevity as the leading macro trend that is shaping their firms. Of those financial advisers who recognize the importance of longevity, 44 percent expect that longer client lifespans will significantly affect their businesses over the next decade, and they cite the challenge of ensuring that their clients' assets will last throughout their lifetimes.[3]

Longer lifespans and longevity remain important trends in which to integrate the opportunity into a marketing strategy for any type of financial services and wealth management company. Newer companies, many app-focused, have emerged to help people save more and use a budget.[4]

Subdomain: Women Investors and Financial Literacy

"Understanding longevity made us better at serving our clients," says Andy Sieg, president of Merrill Lynch Wealth Management.[5] Sieg says the lens he and his colleagues use when thinking about customers and products is what drives happiness and satisfaction in later life, rather than what the customers will need to get through a certain number of years.

By investing in understanding the market, the company has also identified even more opportunities in subdomains and different segmentations. In 2018, Merrill Lynch identified a $1 million wealth gap between women and men by the time both reach current retirement age. Three factors contribute to this gap: the wage gap, women's greater likelihood of having career interruptions for caregiving, and women's longer average lifespans.[6] From its qualitative and quantitative research, Merrill noticed how many women lamented not having invested more, so the company created tools in the financial literacy subdomain specifically for women to use to prepare for their, frankly, more complex longevity journeys. Increased financial education initiatives for women investors have become a core part of the bank's strategy.

Subdomains: Financial Exploitation and Elder Abuse; Financial Caregiving

In the end-of-life stage, there is, sadly, another growing market for fighting financial abuse of older people. Though you may envision salespeople and other outsiders preying on people in their legacy or end-of-life stages, it's more common for close family members to be the perpetrators of financial exploitation. I have personally witnessed families being destroyed when some family members take advantage of vulnerable older adults and their unsuspecting relatives.

Estimates vary widely, but at least $9 billion and as much as $30 billion of wealth is stolen every year through this kind of exploitation and undue influence. Nearly 98 percent of cases go unreported;

only one in forty-four are referred to adult protective services or the authorities.

Two key definitions are helpful in understanding this problem.

According to the National Center for Injury Prevention and Control, *financial abuse or exploitation* is defined as follows: "The illegal, unauthorized, or improper use of an older individual's resources by a caregiver or other person in a trusting relationship, for the benefit of someone other than the older individual. This includes depriving an older person of rightful access to, information about, or use of, personal benefits, resources, belongings, or assets. Examples include forgery, misuse or theft of money or possessions; use of coercion or deception to surrender finances or property; or improper use of guardianship or power of attorney."[7]

The American Bar Association and National Center on Law and Elder Rights defines *undue influence* this way: "When people use their role and power to exploit the trust, dependency, and fear of others. They use this power to deceptively gain control over the decision making of the second person."[8]

Although financial institutions are working with law enforcement to identify fraud, there is a need for more ways to educate families and caregivers about the risk factors associated with this unique type of fraud, which often goes undiscovered until after the victim has died. As adults age, written and valid advance directives, power of attorney, and transparency become paramount as prevention tools.

It's hard to talk about this topic as an opportunity, but there is a serious need for products and services to benefit both the person who is the target of such abuse and the people in that person's life. Many small companies are emerging in a new subdomain we might call *financial caregiving*. They include True Link, Everplans, Silver Bills, Golden, Eversafe, and FreeWill. Some of these companies will take money management out of the target's hand to do bill paying, for example, so that money isn't accessible to others. Or they will alter the flow of funds by, for example, providing prepaid debit cards at intervals to control how much money is available at any one time.

How Nike Is Discovering the Older Athlete

Many companies' strategies start and end with the eighteen- to thirty-four-year-old demographic. This was especially true of Nike, a global market leader that built a $37 billion empire selling athletic footwear and apparel, mostly to that demographic.

In 2019, Nike decided to expand its strategy to address the needs of older athletes who made up 10 percent of the company's sales and who spent more per purchase than other customers did. Quite deliberately, Nike didn't decide to create sneakers for older people but instead aimed specifically for *athletes getting older*. Mike Spillane, then president of Categories and Product at Nike, began a process of understanding Nike's longevity customer, who may have been an active or competitive runner and who now is a "slow runner." He also knew that many older people walk for exercise (more than 110 million Americans walk for fitness, and 60 million jog), but Nike's target was, again, deliberately not the older walker. It was the older athlete who walked. He wanted to find a way to capture the product loyalty Nike had developed over the years and focus it on those who still view themselves as athletes. The company's goal was to capture the "athlete forever" and "continuous athlete."[9]

Nike engineered a new product launched as the CruzrOne. It was designed specifically with famed Nike founder Phil Knight in mind—himself the customer in the continuous-athlete stage. The shoe was designed by legendary sneaker designer Tinker Hatfield. It targeted runners at or above a thirteen-minutes-per-mile pace. Nike redesigned the heel, midsole, and forefoot to cause the landing weight to be further back on the heel and to encourage a forward rolling movement, helping the "slow runner" preserve momentum. Despite this design, Nike's messaging notably did not highlight these features or the observation that the buyer was now a slow runner. Nike's marketing was focused on the stage, the continuous athlete, who doesn't think of themselves as needing help but will appreciate a product that provides it.

The CruzrOne was launched online only as a pilot, selling for $150 per pair. It's no longer part of a separate division within Nike. Even as the company understood and started marketing to the continuous athlete, it continued to evolve its strategy. In July 2020, Nike shifted to a new consumer segmentation, simply, men, women, and kids. Mike Spillane became the president of Consumer Creation, which includes all three new divisions. In the first two categories, he is integrating the continuous-athlete paradigm across the lifespan, as Nike continues to recognize the growing market of "athletes forever" and that a full third of its customers could fall into this category within a couple of decades. Older consumers value product loyalty, and Nike is positioned to create it.

The key for Nike has been to avoid a broad definition of the target market—the company didn't target the huge swath of walkers or people only focused on fashion. The company initially focused on a specific subdomain in a specific stage. Nike also left assumptions and biases at the door. Rather than saying "This is what older people need in a shoe," the company listened to how its customers *defined themselves* and led with that. "You don't have to be the consumer, but you have to understand the consumer," Spillane says. "Being a good listener is the essence of good marketing practice."

Nike is now focusing on a broader definition of sport and broader definition of athlete, to include the sport forever and athlete forever themes, and additional ways to keep the older demographic active. It is developing a deeper products strategy around future fitness, such as viewing dance and yoga as a sport and apparel strategy for this group. The company also sees an opportunity to become a leading voice in the public health discussion about helping people create longer healthspans through an active lifestyle.

Company: Nike

Domains: fitness; apparel

Subdomain: the continuous athlete

Opportunity: $4 billion, and growing, shoe market

Stages addressed: repurposing, renaissance, optimizing health

Best practices: markets products to its core client—athletes—instead of marketing to the demographic of older adults; develops longer loyalty of athletes beyond age brackets of the younger consumer; focuses on a specific stage and segment

How Warby Parker Moved beyond Hipsters

Warby Parker was established in February 2010 and, like many socially minded ventures of the time, donated a pair of glasses to someone in need for every pair it sold. At the outset, cofounders Neil Blumenthal and Dave Gilboa focused on the classic eighteen- to thirty-four-year-old customer base with single-vision prescription lenses at affordable prices. Essentially it offered a $500 product for $95. One tradeoff was variety. A typical optical shop will carry one thousand SKUs. Blumenthal told me that Warby Parker launched with thirty styles in three colors each—a total of ninety SKUs.[10]

In the second year, the company added sunglasses and prescription sunglasses. Year three added new frames in different materials.

Only in the fourth year, when it opened retail stores, did Warby Parker introduce progressive lenses, which correct for more than one field of vision and make the transition from distance correction on top to reading correction on the bottom. Progressive lenses avoid a common situation for many older adults; they need two or more pairs of eyeglasses with different prescriptions.

Warby Parker quickly learned that a huge market for progressive lenses existed. More than half of the eyewear market is progressives in the United States, with an average pair costing $500.

The company had spent three years striving to become a favorite brand of young hipsters, but in year four, it shifted focus to support the longevity market. Specifically, it saw a big opportunity with customers moving to progressive lenses. The company created digital capabilities that enabled longevity customers to obtain important vision measurements without having to visit a store. And although the prescription check app that allows customers to see if their current prescription is correct before renewing a prescription hasn't yet been approved for people over sixty-five, Warby Parker is prepping to provide this capability when it is approved. The company has put effort into making digital and in-store experiences that appeal to this new customer segment.

Another key focus for Warby Parker was to avoid designing new glasses for a different demographic. It put progressive lenses in its existing hip and popular frames—recognizing that people in many stages want fashionable glasses. Warby Parker also determined that this approach would be best to serve people who were changing over to a new type of more complicated eyeglasses—people who, by the way, can be found in many age demographics.

And the company had to do it in a way that served their overall strategy of providing lower-cost alternatives. While marketing direct to consumer often involves high customer acquisition costs in the longevity and health-care markets, Warby Parker found that targeted TV and Facebook ads were effective in reaching its target market of customers moving to progressive lenses. Thus, it can charge on average $295 for progressive lenses.

Embracing this market means the company has also initiated some subtler changes to its advertising strategy. For example, it includes older adults in its ads. Blumenthal emphasized that one of the challenges now is to insure age diversity of models in advertising in general.[11]

Pivoting to support this market became so successful that Warby Parker now identifies itself as not just for the young and hip but also as a company that proudly offers multigenerational products. Progressives now constitute nearly 30 percent of revenues, with more than a million pairs of glasses with progressive lenses sold between 2014 and 2019.

With the increased usage and authorization for telemedicine reimbursement by Medicare and most health insurers, Warby Parker has discovered its longevity strategy. By attracting customers to a brand associated with youth, it has extended its brand to an older customer and has tailored products to help serve customers with different needs. Its goals are now to have decades-long and multigenerational customers.

Company: Warby Parker

Domain: eyewear

Subdomain: progressive lenses

Opportunity: $10–$15 billion in the United States

Stages addressed: transition, portfolio, renaissance, sidepreneur, legacy

Best practices: developed multigenerational marketing campaigns; pricing strategy tailored to longevity customers; enhanced digital portal to serve longevity customers

What Merrill Lynch, Nike, and Warby Parker Did Right

If we zoom out, we can see a few common themes in these cases. These common approaches will help you in the domains and subdomains you look at.

First, focus. None of the companies went big and broad. Nike, for example, didn't target everyone who wears sneakers over a certain age. Yes, that would be a lot more people than continuous athletes—the subdomain it did target—but such a group is not a viable one to market to; there's simply too much diversity of stages within that group to do it.

Many companies, like Merrill Lynch, expand their longevity strategy to many products and many stages once they've identified a subdomain for their marketing efforts. Merrill Lynch added one specific consumer in one stage in one subdomain when they focused on women in the renaissance stage and financial planning products.

Second, while the products and services were designed for longevity customers, the companies didn't necessarily treat those features as the sellable aspects of the offering. Warby Parker didn't market the progressives as different eyeglasses for different people. It positioned them as the same stylish ones hipsters love with lenses that people in the longevity market needed. Likewise, Nike targeted athletes first, but it just so happened that they were athletes at a certain stage.

Third, serving the longevity market does not mean shying away from technology. Perhaps one of the most misunderstood aspects of this market is the demographics' relationship to technology. The key for marketers is to use the technology in ways that serve the customer, and not assume longevity customers are digitally naive. They may want it simpler, but they will use technology.

Finally, those who research and delve into the longevity market often discover the benefits of applying their ideas within their own organization—as Merrill Lynch did by offering its own employees caregiving benefits.

Many companies are surprised to find that the hardest thing about the longevity market is just choosing to participate. Once you enter, focusing on stage, not age, the possibilities open up.

New and Nontraditional Strategies

Spotting opportunities in your existing markets, as the companies just profiled have done, is a good starting point, but new and sometimes unexpected opportunities will arise from longer lifespans and healthspans. One of the most important new strategies will emerge around a changing sentiment about *where* people in this demographic want to live. More than 90 percent of Americans say they would prefer to age in place as they grow older, rather than move to a continuing care retirement community, an assisted living facility, or a nursing home. Given the growing number of people with longer healthspans, we can expect the number of longevity customers who age in place to grow significantly.

Domain: Aging in Place

Often, this domain is described as aging on the go, or thriving in the home. There are easily more than twenty-five subdomains within this incredible potential market, which is estimated at $750 billion. Subdomains include housing, social isolation, transportation and mobility, wellness and fitness, and home modification to name a few.

Many of these will overlap, and some may not be obvious, as we'll see. Take home remodeling. Modifications to homes to allow aging in place, and building new homes designed for aging in place, are huge opportunities just waiting to be snatched up. While there are more than 650,000 remodelers in the United States, less than 1 percent of them are certified for aging in place.[12] The building and remodeling subdomains will overlap with tech companies developing smart features for homes. The tech subdomain creates opportunities in UX and monitoring services. Technology may also enter into kitchen appliances, yet another area that will evolve to help people age in place. Some in the longevity industry are defining these domains and subdomains under the umbrella term *age tech*. Technology is clearly transforming aging in place and affects virtually every domain and subdomain we describe. However, we still need to understand the many segments therein.

We profile these different subdomains all related to aging in place and all having an age-tech component to their strategy: social isolation, alternative housing, transportation and mobility, telehealth, digital health, wellness and fitness, and home improvement.

Subdomain: Social Isolation

Social isolation carries a health consequence equivalent to smoking fifteen cigarettes per day and exceeds the health risks associated with obesity.[13] It is defined as the gap between the social connections you would like to have and those you feel you experience. In 2017, the US surgeon general, Vivek Murthy, called loneliness a public health epidemic.[14] The United Kingdom appointed a "minister for loneliness" a year later. Loneliness hits older people living alone especially hard. They engage in less healthy behaviors and find themselves readmitted into hospitals more often than do their peers who don't feel socially isolated.

Isolation is the catch with aging in place. On the one hand, it's healthy for people to age in place as much as they can, but on the other hand, they lose some of the social connections they would get in care facilities and communities. Companies are emerging to reestablish social connections to combat the isolation that can come with aging in place.

Wider Circle was formed by two entrepreneurs to bring together neighbors to exercise, socialize, and improve their own well-being in groups of ten to twelve. Trained facilitators and member ambassadors lead regular meetings and outings and provide transportation.[15]

There's no cost to the individual; membership is sponsored and paid for by Medicare Advantage plans. The goal initially was to reduce costs to Medicare and to lower hospital admissions. The program has done that: compared with nonmembers, Wider Circle members were admitted 27 percent less frequently to a hospital; spent 43 percent fewer days in the hospital; and have 12 percent more annual wellness visits and 32 percent more flu vaccinations.

But the program has turned out to be a powerful marketing vehicle for the Medicare Advantage plans, too. Darin Buxbaum, one of the cofounders, told me that the members trust the program, which encourages renewal and word-of-mouth new sign-ups.[16] Trust, it turns out, is a key element to successful marketing to older adults.

Wider Circle's solution for loneliness was effective and correct, but its initial underlying hypothesis for its business strategy was not complete. The Covid-19 pandemic threw new challenges at Wider Circle, but the company developed online capabilities to compensate for the inability to meet in person. It also began a program whereby its ambassadors would check in on members, and it partnered with Uber to have meals delivered to homebound older adults. After the company created four new programs and expanded beyond California into Georgia and Michigan, revenue doubled in one month.

The key for Wider Circle was recognizing that its business was not providing classes and social events. It was giving people an enhanced purpose and meaning, one of the key determinants of successful aging as defined by Philip Pizzo's "prescription for longevity."[17] We can help older people find purpose and meaning in many ways, in person and virtually.

Startup companies are recognizing the opportunity of Medicare Advantage plans as both a new customer for them and a channel for distribution of their products and services to others. It requires a focused effort on marketing to distinct groups (user and customer) but the payoff is there. A more detailed discussion of Medicare Advantage is found in chapters 5 and 6.

Company: Wider Circle

Domain: aging in place

Subdomains: social isolation and loneliness; social determinants of health

Opportunity: $7 billion; one-third of older adults feel lonely, and 25 percent are socially isolated; affects health outcomes and associated costs for more than 50 million Americans

Stages addressed: transition through legacy

Best practices: markets its services to Medicare Advantage plans; created community among the end users by forming "circles of care"

Subdomain: Alternative Housing

The desire to age successfully in one's own home and not in a retirement or senior housing community has generated greater attention to new alternatives for housing and opportunities for home modifications. Traditional approaches to housing have included several successful businesses that specialize in building so-called senior housing. These companies, such as Seniorly and A Place for Mom, are profiled in chapter 6.

But there are other, somewhat surprising, markets emerging because people who want to age in place are in all different stages. One growing trend is in intergenerational housing. Older adults with space in their homes are matched with younger roommates. With this simple step, the younger person gains affordable housing while also combating isolation and loneliness for the homeowner. The roommate can often also provide tech assistance, shopping, and other services.

One company supporting intergenerational housing in several major cities is Silvernest, which provides a matching system, lease management, and localized support services. Additional services and infrastructure can be tacked on through such local organizations as the Village to Village Network. Started on Beacon Hill in Boston, the organization creates "villages" of connected seniors who can share resources in neighborhoods.

Add-on services from other companies makes Silvernest a platform play. Suddenly, growth isn't dependent only on the company's ability to come up with new offerings itself. Now the company can vet and add services from other companies, much as you add an app on a smartphone.

Others are building platforms, too. Nesterly has created a platform to match older adults with younger roommates and conducts full background checks. During the Covid-19 pandemic, it partnered with the City of Boston for a free service that connects at-risk individuals with volunteers to fulfill basic needs, including no-contact deliveries and friendly check-ins. UpsideHōM provides furnished apartments and, depending on the customer's stage, food delivery, transportation, activities, and more.

The platform play is smart because it can adapt as people move through multiple stages while aging in place.

Company: Silvernest, Nesterly, UpsideHōM

Domain: aging in place

Subdomains: alternative housing; home improvement

Opportunity: $2 billion

Stages addressed: transition, renaissance, caregiving, legacy

Best practices: creating housing alternatives for older adults while addressing the loneliness factor and simultaneously creating community and a platform in which to offer a range of desired services

Subdomains: Social Isolation; Transportation; Mobility; Telehealth

Just as social networks all link to each other, we're starting to see platforms connect to platforms in longevity. Take Papa, a technology platform that enables college and nursing students to help older adults with transportation, home chores, technology lessons, and other services. While initially a platform for companionship and support for older adults, Papa now also partners with assisted living communities and offers a network of board-certified and licensed physicians, nurse practitioners, and behavioral health specialists to provide telehealth services. Papa also joined forces with Uber Health to further ensure transportation is not a barrier to timely medical appointments. In November 2021, Papa announced expanded offerings to include an additional twenty-six health plans that offer Papa services to their enrollees and a $150 million Series D raise. The platform continues to expand with its Papa Pals serving members in all fifty states and across Medicare Advantage, Medicaid, and employer health plans such as Humana and Aetna.

As these platforms start to join forces and integrate, they're creating an *intergenerational care system.* Key to success as these platforms work together will be identifying the multiple types of customers at different stages, finding products and services that plug into the platform for those customers, and identifying all the different payers. Papa illustrates that it can work with a range of customers through Medicare Advantage, assisted living providers, health plans, and innovative housing communities such as UpsideHōM.

The emergence of telehealth services during the Covid-19 pandemic is a remarkable shift that will continue to grow in the longevity economy. It has obviated the need for some transportation services, but older adults will continue to need transportation at certain life stages. The ability to travel will also help combat the isolation faced by those staying in their homes. People will still need to get to medical appointments, social events, religious services, workplace, or volunteer opportunities. This market opportunity alone is estimated to be about $4 billion.

Companies such as Uber and Lyft have created new verticals to address the needs of the older rider. Uber Health has formed partnerships with more than a thousand health-care organizations to provide medical transportation. The platform created age-friendly tools, apps, and phone systems. It also joined forces with NimbleRx to offer prescription drug delivery.

Similarly, Lyft Health enables health providers to directly order Lyft rides from their electronic medical record system such as Epic. It has extended its services to include Lyft Concierge, which benefits older adults, and has collaborated with assisted living and senior communities.

Though they constitute a smaller subset in certain stages, some older adults are uncomfortable with mobile tech and apps. A company like GoGoGrandparent seizes on this opportunity to simplify the process of ordering an Uber or a Lyft without an app. It further enables family notification of pickup and drop-off times and advanced scheduling for fixed appointments. GoGoGrandparent has added meal and grocery delivery as well.

Some key insights here include using technology to facilitate standard tasks and creating networks of knowledge for care. The ability to notify family caregivers provides a valuable service to another customer who may be younger. Linking to medical record systems is a clever way to gain insight and create efficient delivery of services.

Company: Papa, Uber Health, Lyft Health, GoGoGrandparent

Domain: aging in place

Subdomains: social isolation; mobility; transportation

Opportunity: more than $4 billion

Stages addressed: transition through end of life

Best practices: expanded services beyond transportation services; companionship to address loneliness; extensions into health-care offerings

Subdomains: Telehealth; Digital Health

Telehealth is perhaps one of the better-developed markets in longevity. An indicator of the value in this market came in 2020, when Teledoc, a service offered in 170 countries and with eleven million visits in the past five years, acquired Livongo, a digital platform for diabetes management, for $18.5 billion.[18]

In some ways, this subdomain includes sub-subdomains. Entirely new economic models to support care are being created. Telehealth may enable, for example, *hospital at home*, in which someone can recover from a procedure at home rather than in a hospital, through sensor technology and telehealth services. You can see multiple opportunities just within this concept, whether you develop the technology to support this idea or provide the actual service by creating a network of caregivers.

Tailoring these concepts to the needs of the caregiver and care recipient is both an innovation gap and a market opportunity. As we will see in the next section, caregivers may in fact become health providers in the home and will consequently need a host of innovations to support that role.[19]

The pandemic has accelerated the development and, frankly, acceptance of telehealth. This is an exploding opportunity.

Company: Teledoc, Tembo Health

Domain: aging in place

Subdomain: telehealth

Opportunity: $250 billion

Stages addressed: caregiving through end of life

Best practices: specialty care focused on the needs of the older patient, with professionals who uniquely understand the complexities of coordinating care

Subdomains: Wellness; Fitness Training

Another subdomain is wellness and a new sub-subdomain to telehealth is online fitness training. The success of companies like Peloton means there's a growing acceptance of exercise and fitness delivered remotely. One company, Bold, offers a remote strength test and then designs a twelve-week fitness program based on the assessment for older adults. The goal of fitness is a longer healthspan but also, quite specifically, to reduce falls. One in three adults over sixty-five falls every year. The care costs from falls are $50 billion annually.

Company: Bold

Domains: digital health; aging in place

Subdomains: wellness; fitness

Opportunity: $50 billion

Stages addressed: optimizing health through renaissance

Best practices: online training program customized to the needs of individuals; partnerships with health plans

Subdomain: Home Improvement

In terms of home improvements, renovation and tech upgrades are big opportunities. The National Association of Home Builders has begun offering the Certified Aging-in-Place Specialist (CAPS) program. The association provides an aging-in-place checklist that includes specifications to support older adults. The specs include details like thirty-six-inch-wide doors, wider hallways, nonslip flooring, lever handles on doors and faucets, and low- or no-threshold doorways. (Several Scandinavian countries have implemented universal design principles to all new building construction to enhance healthy aging.) So far only a few builders are CAPS certified, specialize in building to specs designed for aging in place, or provide products and services to adapt homes. Since the majority of renovations are done by people over fifty, home improvement and home building for longevity are highly untapped opportunities.

. . .

Additional domains sometimes fall under the umbrella of aging in place but are so significant that they constitute their own domain and even their own economy. Next we profile the caregiving economy and its many subdomains.

The Caregiving Economy

Caregiving is a traditional market domain but it is so vast and is changing so much that it deserves its own exploration. Caregiving alone is nearly a $1 trillion market.

This domain concerns two key segments: nonprofessional family caregivers and professional caregivers. More than 53 million Americans provided unpaid care in 2020 to more than 48 million older adults.[20] The value of that family caregiving is $470 billion. The market for professional caregiving is $500 billion.[21] The numbers are similarly huge around the world.

Hundreds of new companies have emerged in these domains and many subdomains, including care navigation and transition support services, care coordination, caregiver quality of life, daily essential activities for the care recipient, wearables, fall prevention and detection, and financial caregiving. The appendix contains details about each of the more than twenty-six subdomains associated with caregiving. And as is the case for many of the longevity innovations that we have examined so far, there are multiple opportunities for any one company because the needs of, and opportunities in, this market overlap.

Those looking to serve this market must appreciate its complexity. In any one subdomain, there will be multiple stakeholders—care providers, care recipients, coordinators, influential family members, the purchaser, the payer. All these roles may be different people or they may overlap.

Caregiving is both a stage for older adults and a significant domain in longevity. It includes many caregiving tasks beyond what you might expect. For example, grandparents caring for children are part of the caregiving market. A person in the renaissance stage may also be in the caregiving stage for a spouse or partner who needs some care. A person in their forties may be in the caregiving stage and is part of this longevity market.

Care for children, that is, parenting, is a well-developed market with a plethora of content and products to help parents. No such comprehensive literature or market exists for other kinds of caregiving, including that provided for older adults. Caregiving for children is a largely linear march to independence, but caregiving for older adults is a more complex, fractured affair. It is common to go from one new crisis to another, usually with new medical needs and different kinds of support and care needed. Primarily unpaid caregivers are not trained to handle this progression. For this reason, caregiving is a major market opportunity.

For example, consider this profile of my caregiving stages: The first time I was a caregiver for my father was when I was a teenager. I was a caregiver for my widowed mother at different times over a period of two decades in my thirties through my fifties. At no time did I really have the tools and knowledge I needed to fully understand the different types of care they needed. Moreover, no one ever marketed their products and services to me.

New platforms are needed to close huge gaps in the caregiving domain and its subdomains, including a platform that aids families in curating information and resources and in navigating care. Several new companies providing important care navigation and transition support are marketing to health-care plans and to employers that offer this as a benefit to their employees, who may be juggling their own work and parental or spousal care responsibilities. The payers in these examples are neither the end user nor the care recipient.

So significant is the need for innovations for caregiving that Pivotal Ventures, the investment and incubation company created by Melinda French Gates to advance social progress in the United States, announced in January 2020 the launch of a multiyear initiative in partnership with Techstars, an investor and accelerator for startups. Together, they established a new program called the Future of Longevity Accelerator. This first-of-its-kind accelerator focuses solely on innovation and creative caregiving solutions to address the unmet needs of older adults and their caregivers.[22]

The accelerator incubates ten companies each year in a thirteen-week program. Each company receives a $120,000 investment and has access to multiple mentors throughout the development of its startup. I have been one of the accelerator's lead mentors and currently serve as a mentor in residence. The twenty companies to come through thus far in the 2020 and 2021 classes focus on many of the caregiving domains discussed here. Most of the entrepreneurs in these accelerator classes have had a personal family experience that inspired them to solve a caregiving need. A goal for this accelerator is to advance solutions empowering older adults to live with greater well-being and dignity, while alleviating the pressures on people who care for them.[23]

The following profiled companies illustrate new approaches and business strategies. Each of these companies addresses a different component of the market and the varied needs associated with caregiving. Each has a different business model and customer acquisition strategy.

There is plenty of market share left—no one company can serve the myriad needs of the entire market, and there will be regional differences that influence your strategy. Rural communities, for example, represent a unique opportunity that will benefit from solutions that address the aspects of delivering caregiving in widely spread-out areas with limited connectivity.

In fact, there are more than twenty subdomains related to caregiving. While we profile some here, we can't address them all. Resources for a more complete analysis of the caregiving economy and landscape of caregiving innovations are included in the appendix.[24]

Subdomains: In-Home Care; Technology

Serial entrepreneur Seth Sternberg founded Honor in 2014 to provide training for home providers and to smooth the supply of trained and reliable caregivers. Honor initially saw the care professionals as its product, selling directly to those who needed professional caregiving. But that approach quickly morphed as the company targeted this domain and its many subdomains. Company leaders realized that the hyperlocal nature of the caregiving market meant they could do better by also focusing on such services as care plans and client profiles for the *suppliers* of care professionals—the hundreds of local care agencies. By incorporating artificial intelligence (AI) into its business strategy to predict demand for caregiving, Honor reduced turnover of care providers from 80 to 30 percent.

The shift from marketing to consumers to marketing to local agencies paid off and created a level of trust with the agencies. This in turn allowed Honor to start exploring other caregiving subdomains, such as transportation. It created partnerships with Uber and local supermarkets for food delivery services.

Honor now describes its strategy as a home-care technology company that works with local agencies to provide reliable, high-quality in-home care. The new strategy was a pivot away from its initial direct-to-consumer model. In August 2021, Honor announced it had acquired Home Instead, one of the largest home-care networks and will integrate their home-care technology and operations platform. The combined organization now represents more than $2.1 billion in revenue. Honor's success offers a good lesson that in a market like this, being open to new ideas and business models is essential, especially for a startup. The company recognized that in this highly fragmented market, Honor had to establish a trusted channel and a trusted relationship.

Company: Honor

Domain: caregiving

Subdomains: paid in-home care; technology and operations support platform

Opportunity: $9–$500 billion

Stage: caregiving

Best practices: made the caregiving supply chain more dynamic and responsive through technology; addressed the hyperlocal nature of the paid home-care ecosystem; integrated a large provider and network of personal home care

Subdomains: Care Coordination; Navigation

Whether the task is helping nonpaid family members juggle work, care, and the rest of their lives or helping professionals plan and effectively provide services, care coordination is a gaping hole in the longevity market. A company called Vesta Healthcare entered this realm initially by marketing to home-care aides. It struggled to grow with that target customer. So the company shifted the care model to market to the network of providers as a unit—the care aides, family caregivers, and health providers. Vesta built tech that allowed the network of caregivers to share information and insights. Communication is huge in the coordination of care, and this approach is meant to facilitate communication.

The company has focused specifically on high-need, frail, older-adult populations. Through telehealth, a clinician can monitor the health of the care recipient, while caregivers—whether they are pros or family members—can link to talk to nurses to discuss situations. CEO Randy Klein says the tech helps caregivers "coach to resolution" half of the time and avoid emergency department use and hospital admission and readmissions, a common and costly experience for frail older adults.[25]

Klein attributes some of Vesta's success to its focus on the caregiver and treating caregivers with respect. Too often, he believes, companies fail because they "patronize" caregivers, especially nonprofessionals.

By treating them as partners in the network, Vesta has built trust with this group.

Company: Vesta Healthcare

Domain: caregiving

Subdomains: care coordination; care navigation; telehealth

Opportunity: $30 billion

Stage addressed: caregiving

Best practices: provides a trusted partner in caregiving, with telehealth 24-7 support to prevent hospitalizations, and values and integrates the insights of the caregiver with the entire care team

Subdomains: Transition Planning; Care Navigation

One of the most stressful parts of caregiving for family members is planning transitions, whether it's moving a loved one into care facilities or an adult child's home or finding in-home caregivers. The transition is complicated. It involves many decisions and takes time and energy.

So it makes sense that this is an opportunity to help caregivers manage all this. But a company like Wellthy is doing it by selling the service not just to caregivers but also to their employers. After her own difficult experience as a caregiver, Lindsay Jurist-Rosner cofounded Wellthy to provide concierge services, including private care coordinators, to caregivers as an employee benefit.[26] For families with aging members, the company provides assistance with finding an in-home aide or handling a move into a facility; recommending local socialization programs; setting up home modifications, meal delivery, and transportation; finding the right legal resources, including establishing powers of attorney; and navigating Medicare, Medicare Advantage, social security, and veteran's benefits.

Wellthy markets these services as good for the business and the care-giver. Helping caregivers means increased productivity and "presen-teeism," increased employee loyalty, improved retention of high-value employees, and alleviation of employees' unspoken stress.

The area of employer-benefit space will be growing, as more employ-ees face the dual challenge of childcare and parent care while working and building their own careers. Wellthy has also expanded to selling their services to Medicare Advantage, health plans, and insurers.

Company: Wellthy

Domain: caregiving

Subdomains: care navigation; transition planning

Opportunity: more than $30 billion

Stages addressed: parenting/family; caregiving

Best practices: addressing the challenges employees and employers face while working and having family caregiving re-sponsibilities by providing an employer benefit that includes a caregiving concierge service

A few themes have emerged in the broad caregiving domain. Those entering this market will be serving many stages and often people who are not the target of the care. There is a tremendous opportu-nity in connecting the dots for people—coordinating care, planning for predictable events that too many people don't know about until the event is upon them, and offloading stressful decision-making to experts. Also, technology will be pervasive in caregiving, whether it is through telehealth that allows remote consultations with experts, sensors that track the condition of the person receiving care, or even AI to predict where the market is going. Expect platforms to grow in this space as well.

Another broad domain that impacts every family and is part of the longevity market is end-of-life care and planning. Profiled here are several companies who are taking different approaches to this $170 billion market.

Domain: End-of-Life Care and Planning

Death and dying are life events that require a variety of actions and create the need for assistance and guidance for an individual and family members. It can be an overwhelming time if there is no plan in place or no clear understanding of the dying person's wishes.

During the Covid-19 pandemic, the need to plan for end-of-life care became urgent, and news organizations wrote weekly about its importance. In recent years, the concept of having a good death has been promoted by the Institute of Medicine, which encourages planning, documenting, and adhering to the wishes of the person who will die. According to the institute, a good death is "one that is free from avoidable distress and suffering, for patients, family, and caregivers; in general accord with the patients' and families' wishes; and reasonably consistent with clinical, cultural, and ethical standards."[27]

Too often the dignity and preferences of the dying person are compromised because of a lack of planning. Families can disintegrate over conflicts related to the many aspects of death and the decisions it requires. Death is a medical event, a legal event, a financial event, a spiritual event, an emotional and family event, and a legacy event. Each of these aspects of death generates different needs and opportunities.

Despite everyone's desire for a good death for their family member and themselves, such a death is not that common. More than three in five Americans lack end-of-life plans. Four of five haven't spoken about funeral arrangements. Although 90 percent of people want to die at home, only 30 percent do.

It turns out that end-of-life care and planning is another longevity market opportunity that is surprisingly large and fragmented. The need for palliative care and hospice is estimated to be a $30 billion market opportunity. The advance care planning opportunity exceeds $50 billion.

Funeral and burial services, including new green alternatives, exceeds $21 billion in the United States.

Each of these needs is a part of the many different subdomains of the end-of-life care market opportunity. The companies profiled here are among those that are addressing the needs of families and have successfully understood the complexities of this market.

Companies like the platform called Cake are looking to tackle nearly every aspect of the end of life, including advance funeral arrangements, the appointing of a decision maker, and becoming a repository for documents and planning.[28] In addition, it provides tools to help people navigate the expected emotional toll of grief and loss from a death.

Such an ambitious approach requires partnerships, from which Cake receives a referral and a revenue-sharing fee. The company initially began selling its platform to businesses such as financial institutions and health-care payers and providers, who paid a license fee (anywhere from $10,000 to $1 million) for access over three years. Those customers would in turn offer Cake's services to their customers.

But in 2019, Cake founder and CEO, Suelin Chen, introduced a direct-to-consumer model because the long sales cycles of working with companies were inhibiting growth. This approach, which relies on smart search engine optimization to acquire customers, was successful in generating leads, most often from women, for both their own families and their parents.

The Covid-19 pandemic also increased Cake's visibility. "The pandemic sped up existing trends in consumer views on end of life," Chen says. "We've seen increased demand and decreased stigma around these topics—it is now seen as an essential part of people's health and financial wellbeing."[29]

Still, Chen advises that "this field is nascent, and . . . there are so many areas to navigate. Every family will need this multiple times."

Company: Cake

Domains: end-of-life care and planning; post-loss support

Subdomains: palliative care and hospice; advance care planning; legal planning; funerals and burials; legacy planning; grief and loss

Opportunity: more than $100 billion

Stages addressed: parenting/family through end of life

Best practices: created a platform that offers the complete range of services and products potentially needed in end-of-life care and planning; identified both corporate customers and a direct-to-consumer strategy

Other companies are focused on more specific parts of end-of-life planning, such as palliative care and hospice—a $31 billion market and growing as more patients prefer not to die in a hospital. Companies like Iris Healthcare are trying to create services in this area not just for the individual and families but also for insurers and health-care providers. In Iris Healthcare's case, they use telehealth and dedicated guides to lead conversations and facilitate decisions about this care. They use a predictive modeling based on claims data to find likely candidates for their services.

Company: Iris Healthcare

Domain: end-of-life care and planning

Subdomains: advance care planning; telehealth

Opportunity: $50 billion

Stages addressed: caregiving through end of life

Best practices: provides concierge-style services to help families begin the difficult process of planning advance care and to ensure that the dying person's wishes are documented and available to the insurance company and health-care providers, as well as to trusted family members

Another company, FreeWill, offers similar planning tools. It was founded in 2016 by two Stanford Graduate School of Business students who developed online estate-planning software to support and encourage donations to nonprofits. In its first three years, FreeWill had created more than twenty-one thousand wills, with upward of $500 million committed to nonprofit causes.

Along the way, the company had built a unique customer acquisition and revenue model. Users sign up, create a will online, and arrange a donation (if desired) in minutes. After this, the will then just needs notarization. There is no cost to the will maker; instead that cost is absorbed by the more than one hundred charities that partner with FreeWill in return for receiving funding through the tool. FreeWill is now expanding its products and services to include advance health-care directives, financial power of attorney, and serves as an entry point to the planning market and is establishing partnerships with other platforms.

Emerging Opportunities and Nonobvious Markets

Market opportunities in longevity are growing to include new domains and subdomains that may not be obvious at first. But given that the demographic fact of longer lifespans and healthspans will touch nearly every aspect of life, unexpected opportunities will emerge and there will be surprising innovations.

Domain: Lifelong Learning

Areas ripe for innovation include lifelong learning, which is poised to change dramatically as the number of older adults who enjoy a longer healthspan and enroll in classes explodes. The profound shift of who uses school—a group that used to be almost entirely composed of people under thirty—has caused some companies to rename this market from *lifelong learning* to *long-life learning.* Think of it this way. An extra ten years of healthspan for an older adult is 3,652 more days to fill with activities and learning. New learning models and technologies are in development to tailor learning to people in the renaissance, repurposing, and other stages, sidepreneurs, olderpreneurs, and more. Digital literacy products will also emerge, as will models to support workforce reentry after retirement from a first career or after career breaks or sabbaticals for caregiving.

Amava, for example, built a platform to create virtual communities of lifelong learners who sort themselves according to their interests. The original business model, according to Mark Silverman, CEO and founder, was referral fees from partnering organizations that, like Road Scholar and the Smithsonian Institution, attracted customers.[30]

But the company evolved to encompass many of the business models we've explored in this chapter, including partnerships with health plans and other organizations that already serve older adults. The platform has attracted almost two hundred thousand users. Its growth is a testament to the need for information, community, and tools to redefine purpose and engagement for those in transition from their careers and work. Among the programs Amava offers is Designing Your Next, a series to help people in the repurposing stage determine their next moves. Retirement Coaching is another popular offering for those in the transition stage. Seminars on Medicare and Medicare Advantage are also popular. The company has also worked with existing education companies like Coursera and ed2go.

One can imagine any number of new learning products based on any of the stages, not just the transition or continuous learner stages. People in the portfolio stage will want a variety of education opportunities as they explore new avenues, for example.

Company: Amava

Domains: lifelong learning; transition planning

Subdomains: unretirement; purpose

Opportunity: $5 trillion

Stages addressed: continuous learner, repurposing, transition, renaissance, sidepreneur, legacy

Best practices: understands the varied needs of older adults in transition; created a strong content platform and a way for those in transition to form communities ("circles") of people with common interests or goals; provides opportunities to define purpose and discover new communities, two essential components of healthy aging and longevity

Learning opportunities also help combat the isolation and loneliness that often affect older adults, especially those trying to age in place. Many of us have signed up for an online course, webinar, or conference, only to drop out in the middle of the session or series because it's not as satisfying learning alone as when we are part of a learning community. Companies like Gather are tapping this opportunity by creating live group learning. Gather operates as a marketplace, offering content from established institutions such as the Smithsonian and other museums and universities.[31] It works with those organizations to design and deliver content to their subscribers as live and virtual sessions. Gather does *not* use a direct-to-consumer model. Rather, it relies on the memberships of the institutions in its marketplace. It has created a new form of digital membership for world-class museums like the Museum of Modern Art, the Metropolitan Museum of Art, and others, reimagining museum membership as a complimentary offering.

In 2019, Gather hosted thirty-nine thousand learning events. The dominant demographic was adults over fifty. By putting a stage lens on the enrollees, the company could market offerings even more precisely. For example, how many enrollees are portfolio-stage learners, and how many are learning as part of a new work opportunity in their renaissance?

Company: Gather

Domain: continuous learning

Subdomains: lifelong learning; education technology; social isolation

Opportunity: $5 trillion

Stages addressed: transition through legacy

Best practices: designs, delivers, and manages learning experiences for long-life learning; fosters engagement in a community of learners; works with institutions that have had "sticky" relationships with subscribed members

Domain: Work

With longer healthspans, it will become increasingly common for five-generation workforces to exist in a single company. It is now well established that a diverse workforce produces better performance and greater creativity. Several companies and other organizations are addressing the new market opportunity that longevity creates, whether they do so by supporting caregiving sabbaticals or older adults who unretire or shift to a new career as they repurpose. Creative strategies to support workers in different stages will become the norm as work and careers span a sixty-year time frame.

This domain contains many subdomains. For example, Encore.org, founded by Marc Freedman, offers fellowships that place experienced workers in nonprofit organizations. Many older adults will be more focused on mission and less focused on career development in their repurposing, portfolio, and renaissance stages, making them excellent candidates for the nonprofit realm. Encore also pairs these older people with younger workers to create intergenerational connections, which have been shown to create many positive effects. Under their Gen2Gen initiatives, they are also mobilizing over one million adults over fifty to help young people thrive through mentoring, tutoring, increasing literacy skills, advocating for a Caring Corps, and are renaming their company Co-generate.

People in the caregiving stage are another target here. iRelaunch was founded in 2008 to help women reenter the workforce after a career break for caretaking of children. The company's model includes workshops for people to learn about new work tools such as LinkedIn and Slack. iRelaunch also offers sixteen-week paid returnships, during which the "relauncher" receives training, experience, mentoring, and often a permanent position. The companies pay iRelaunch a finder's fee for the returners who enter their workforce.

It's easy to see how this model might be adapted for older adults who are launching into second or third careers and who need reentry into the workforce. The company has evolved to support both men and women and to focus on caregivers who take breaks to care for older adults. Breaks and shifts in careers will be the norm in the longevity economy.

Companies: Encore.org; iRelaunch

Domain: unretirement and reentry

Subdomains: transition planning; retooling; repurposing; relaunching

Opportunity: $5 trillion

Stages addressed: continuous learner through sidepreneur

Best practices: developed paid returnships with companies or nonprofit organizations that want to hire those who have taken career breaks or are in a career transition

Domain: Age Tech

Developing technology that targets older adults is an ecosystem that will blossom. Age tech will touch many other domains and subdomains. We've already seen how sensors and virtual consults are making telehealth the norm, fundamentally changing the economics of caring for older adults.

Voice interface is another area being exploited to develop products that make interacting with technology platforms easier. Smart-home technology will grow and affect home improvement, aging in place, medication management, social networking, and other elements of longevity; the list is long.

Large players such as Samsung, Amazon, and Best Buy see a market opportunity worth seizing. Amazon launched the Alexa Care Hub in 2020. Best Buy created a new vertical for aging in place, and offers a Caring Center with unlimited calls to assist with the use of their tech products. Medicare Advantage plans began covering some in-home technology in 2020 to help older adults remain independent. The use of digital health technologies includes remote monitoring and remote consultation.

Aging, technology, and health will be inextricably linked in the future. This relationship will include an ever-growing array of apps to more sensors in homes and wearables. Even technology as simple as a video conference can help, say, a daughter in the caregiving stage stay in closer touch with her aging parent without taxing travel. Or it could help a person in the legacy stage check with professionals on their health status.

The growth of age tech as its own longevity market domain has been emphasized by companies and organizations devoted to following the trends. These include *Aging and Health Technology Watch*, an online publication established by Laurie Orlov, who regularly publishes reports and articles on this industry; the *Gerontechnologist*, another publication created by Keren Etkin to provide important market analyses; and the new AgeTech Collaborative, sponsored by AARP and its Innovation Labs.

Technology will not only make safety measures more accessible but will also help reduce the stigma of aging. Wearables such as smart watches will replace the emergency-response buttons worn around the neck for many. This wearable technology will also increasingly be embedded in clothing, and new types of fashion for older adults will emerge as new market opportunity.

What Does Identifying Domains and Subdomains Mean for My Business and Employees?

By now it should be clear that the opportunities to support the needs and wants of century-long lives are enormous, diverse, and profound. We've seen themes emerge among the best practices as we've explored just a sliver of the domains and subdomains that will be available to you. These themes include the following:

- Applying technology to create new products or more efficient business models, even in places where doing so may not seem obvious

- Thinking creatively and carefully about who the customer is, and pivoting business models to discover new opportunities

- Staying focused on particular stages, segments, and subdomains, and recognizing that although platforms will allow you to expand, it pays to start out more narrowly focused

- Partnering instead of creating; learning that other companies exist and that it's better to find your unique value, and then use other companies for their expertise, than it is to try to reinvent what they already do well

With these cases and this review serving as a basis, I hope you've been inspired to start building a longevity strategy. You know how many opportunities there are and who the customers are. Now you need to reach them.

● RECOMMENDATIONS

- Every company will need to have a longevity strategy for its products and services and workforce.

- Incorporate the over-sixty demographic even if you are a large company with an established brand.

- Identify your strategy using stage and not age.

- Reexamine your product or service strategy with the longevity stage lens, and the strategy will be enhanced to meet the varied needs of the longevity customer.

- Remember that not all needs are for frail older adults or people in the end-of-life stage, but many needs will span a hundred-year life.

- Recognize the diversity in how we age—older adults are a hetero-geneous population with varied needs and wants.

- To be successful companies will need to offer multigenerational products with good design, stealth accommodations, and a strong brand image.

- Infuse older sensitivity into products and design teams.

- Remember that the longevity customer and the end user may in fact be different from the payer or purchaser of your product or service.

CHAPTER 5

Identifying the Customer

Products and services for the longevity market will need to accommodate a multigenerational customer base. More than in other markets, the end user, the customer, and the payer will vary, sometimes being three separate entities for one product. Significantly, at certain stages, an unpaid caregiver such as a family member will more often influence or actually purchase the product or service. Marketers must also recognize and eliminate ageist approaches to marketing.

After her divorce, Monica was the primary breadwinner for her family. She started a new catering company, including online sales of her famous cookies. She used the latest technology to scale her business and develop relationships with cost-efficient suppliers. In her precious spare time, she still danced, her favorite activity. Monica is sixty-four and in good health. Her mother is eighty-six, and Monica has just begun to do more to care for her.

What kind of longevity customer is Monica? Trick question. She is actually at least *three* customers.

As an older adult in her sidepreneur or olderpreneur stage, Monica needs learning products to build her business acumen and she needs technology to run the business. She will need space for operations, and perhaps there will be some adjustments to that space to accommodate an older adult.

But she's also in her third life quarter, the renaissance stage; her priorities don't center solely on accumulating wealth or creating financial security. Dance is important to her, and she invests time in this activity. She wants ways to connect with like-minded peers and build a community around dance.

Monica is also beginning a caregiving stage. As a customer here, she'll be making decisions for someone else, and she may or may not be paying. She'll need education about insurance and programs like Medicare and Medicare Advantage and how they work. She may have to learn about and adopt telehealth and other monitoring technology.

Sometimes, she is a direct-to-consumer customer—say, for business insurance. Often she's a payer for a service for someone else—say, in-home care for her mother. At other times, she's a user whom someone or something else pays for—perhaps her insurance covers the cost of health and fitness classes. At still other times, she's just a consultant, for example, making decisions with her mother's doctor. And finally, she's an influencer, maybe a powerful voice for your product in her dance group.

One kind of customer you'll notice she is not: an old customer. There's little about marketing to Monica that has to do with her age, even if the products support someone her age. Focusing on her age not only won't work, but could also be construed as ageist and turn off someone who is so clearly thriving and thinking of themselves as anything but old. In fact, Monica probably thinks her mother is part of a market for older adults while she herself isn't. And in some ways, she's right, as her mother eases into her legacy stage.

Understanding these nuances is the key to understanding the customer and then marketing effectively. You will gain the insight you need by starting the path to any longevity product or service by answering these three questions:

- Who is making the purchasing decision, and who pays?

- Who is the end user, and what are their needs?

- What are the customer acquisition challenges?

One Market, Many Models, Many Customers

When you answer these questions, you end up identifying several models of delivery and several kinds of customers. Each has its own unique attributes. And identifying your models and customers will improve your chances of success in the longevity market. Common delivery models include the following:

- Services purchased by older people: In this usually direct-to-consumer model, marketers will focus on the customers' stages for positioning.

- Services purchased on behalf of older people: This delivery model is sometimes direct-to-consumer, sometimes a proxy purchase. Marketers here must market both to the stage of the user and to who's making the purchase. For example, if you're selling to a daughter who is buying a meal-kit service for her father, you'll need to both understand the nutritional needs and food preferences of the person eating the meals and know what the buyer wants for her father and how that buyer wants to pay, or can pay, for such a service.

- Services traded between older and younger people: In this potentially direct or indirect model, the customer will fluctuate between the young person and the older person. For example, younger people might rent a room from older people. Marketers must focus on two or more people, each of whom is in a different stage.

- Services delivered to future older people: This model is both direct and indirect. Marketers in this model will focus on helping customers understand and envision something the customers may not be experiencing and convince them of the value of investing.

- Services for older people but paid for by society: Usually the customer is not the user, and marketing must take policy into consideration when designing an offering.

Customers who are part of these models include the following:

- **The end user:** The person buys direct. Monica needs a computer for her business, so Monica buys a computer.

- **The purchaser:** This informed financial source may not be the user. For example, the purchaser could be a contractor who is evaluating and buying products to install in a home designed for aging in place.

- **The influencer:** This customer is an informed nonfinancial source, such as a respected person in the target market or someone with a large social platform.

- **The "daughter":** This adult child of, or the caregiver for, an older adult has informal and unpaid responsibility. Though I use the word *daughter* here, because mother-daughter is the most common caregiving dynamic, this customer could be a son, a niece, a nephew, or a friend. The dynamic is such that a younger person is caring for the older person.

- **Employers:** Increasingly, businesses and their CHROs and CFOs will be identified as customers for new benefit providers for a workforce that is employed well beyond the age of sixty. Employees will inevitably demand new caregiving benefits to make their work more productive.

- **Independent health insurers, including Medicare Advantage providers:** These customers are private institutions, a growing set of which are playing in this space. We'll investigate this class of customers later in this chapter.

- **Government services like Medicare and Medicaid:** These customers are similar to the preceding independent institutions but are largely public and have regulations and policy interactions that are more complex.

- **State and local governments:** Municipal institutions as customers have varied rules and regulations depending on location. The demand for improved social services will drive growth in selling into municipalities.

- Health-care providers: These customers are typically caregiving institutions but are also, increasingly, companies facilitating remote care, wellness, and other services. Technology, products, and services are all rapidly emerging here.

The Customer Is (Often) Female

The demographics are clear: in the new longevity paradigm, women will be among the largest target audiences for products and services. They live longer than men. More women live alone through more stages. More age in place. More continue working through several stages. And even beyond older adults, more women tend to be the major purchasers and influencers for their families. Women's predominance in the longevity market does not preclude marketing to men as customers; there are some clear opportunities for any gender in this market. But having a longevity strategy means learning about and marketing to women in the various stages.

One of the clearest examples of marketing to the female longevity customer is Daughterhood, an organization founded in 2015 by Anne Tumlinson. The very name of the organization captures what many daughters and daughters-in-law know: they bear a disproportionate part of the unpaid caregiving for a family member. To be sure, there are many sons who worry about their parents just as much as women do. And many men are as deeply affected as women are by the burden of responsibility and the experience of witnessing their parents' loss of independence and dignity. But the data shows that seven of ten caregivers for older parents are female family members, and five of six assume primary responsibility for the day-to-day labor-intensive duties such as cooking, cleaning, errands, driving to doctor appointments, bathing, and other activities of daily living.[1]

The titles of the free publications on Daughterhood's site bring a knowing smile for those of us who have been caregivers. Among these titles are "A Sibling's Survival Guide," "3 Mantras for Daughterhood," "Navigating Change," "Setting Boundaries," "The Burden of Self-Care," and "It's Not Your Fault." Daughterhood is a new kind of resource for an increasingly common stage of life that nearly every family goes through, yet most go through it alone. Daughterhood also creates social connections regionally to help provide support and share local resources.

Liz O'Donnell created a similar group called Working Daughter, which is based on her book of the same name.[2] Her blueprint for women and men also includes a call to action for business leaders and policy makers. In addition to helpful online resources and products, her company now offers peer-led local groups—complete with facilitation guides for peer leaders who recruit—that meet regularly for support.

Both these organizations are rich with ore to mine, providing a fount of information about products, services, and needs among women of all ages in the caregiving stage. The organization's social networks are a clear opportunity for testing and promoting some of the products and services you will be creating. And they are likely partner targets because they have built expertise in this growing area.

While daughters are often the primary caregivers, the purchasing decision can be even more complex than simply targeting one family member. The target can be difficult to hit, as multiple members of the family can be involved in purchasing decisions, and conflicting opinions are common. Therefore, targeting the whole family as part of your customer acquisition strategy becomes key, but the entry is usually the primary caregiver (often a daughter), even if they're not the primary payer. Groups like Daughterhood and Working Daughter make this an easier cohort to target.

Companies themselves have begun to form their own support groups for employees who are dealing with the challenges of working and caregiving. Merrill Lynch does so, and many more firms will need to follow its lead. By 2050, more than fifty million employees will be juggling work and caregiving needs. Employers underestimate the spectrum of care responsibilities affecting the different demographics in their organization, though the Covid-19 pandemic has opened many eyes to the reality. Companies that provide support for this huge base will gain a competitive advantage on talent acquisition, as Joseph Fuller and Manjari Raman emphasized in "The Caring Company," a report for the Harvard Business School Project on Managing the Future of Work.[3] But those companies will need products and services to provide such benefits, another massive opportunity.

The Customer Is (Sometimes) Multigenerational

Among the new and nontraditional market opportunities are travel and continuous learning. Imagine how many older adults with disposable income would love to take purposeful educational trips with their grandchildren. So you are marketing the trip not only to the payer and attendee (the grandparent) but also to the parent of the grandchild. The parent wants to know if this trip is something their child will enjoy, and the parent may want to join in as well. Marketing to each generation can be different and may in fact involve different distribution channels.

Products that can be used by multiple generations—for example, legacy tools to record family history for future generations or to enable better care such as with MemoryWell—require that their interface work for both older and younger users.

The Customer Is (Increasingly) Sick of Being Stereotyped

The Pew Research Center and AARP conducted a review in 2019 and determined that the older adult demographic is shunned and caricatured in marketing images, a practice that perpetuates unrealistic stereotypes and contributes to ageist views of the older consumer.[4] You may well think, "Not my company," but consider this data:

- Only 35 percent of people seventy-five or older consider themselves old.

- Around 73 percent feel patronized by companies.

- Some 65 percent think businesses do not care about older consumers.

- Around 80 percent say businesses don't market respectfully to them.

Just as photoshopped imagery of models creates unrealistic expectations for young women and beauty, the pervasiveness of marketing and advertising around older adults doing "old people things"—or, more importantly, not doing things they actually *do*—is both problematic and in need of addressing. Marketing to the longevity customer and the customer acquisition process will change dramatically as advertising agencies and their clients update their portrayals of aging. AARP is pushing better images through a partnership with the stock image clearinghouse Getty Images, increasing the number of photos available that show older people running businesses, playing basketball, and hanging out with younger generations.

Another key area of ageism that marketers should focus on is technology. Older adults are more tech-savvy than many assume. The Pew Foundation released a landmark report in 2017 documenting the increasing use of technology by the older consumer.[5] The past decade saw a major shift in internet use by older adults. Broadband access is common, and more than half of older adults own smartphones and use social networks. Those who have not been in a work environment for some time may require supplemental digital literacy efforts, but overall digital literacy was higher than expected, and crucially, the willingness to try new technology was also high. The Covid-19 pandemic also accelerated the use of technology by older adults, who, along with the rest of us, became fluent in Zoom, online food shopping, and more.

For marketers, the assumption that they can't use these channels to communicate and build products and service on is wrong. Innovators will use these channels to access older adults and will trust these adults to navigate the tech.

The Customer (Always) Deserves Better Product Design

Ageism creeps into product design and the resulting marketing of those products. This bias is part of what drives the older customers' feeling of being patronized and the sense that companies don't care about them.

There is a profound mismatch between products built for older people and the products they actually want. And crossing that gap is a major opportunity.

For some products for people in the legacy stage, there's an unwillingness to use products that benefit them, for complex emotional reasons. For example, only 20 percent of people who could benefit from hearing aids seek them out. Just 2 percent of people over sixty-five seek out personal emergency-response technologies—wearables that can call 911 in the event of an accident. Many that do get them refuse to actually use them.

Beyond that, there's the growing cadre of healthy older adults in many stages who simply don't consider themselves old and so aren't interested in products for old people. But these products may in fact serve them well. Part of this reluctance stems from how the products have been designed. They are often created *for* older adults but not *with* older adults. It seems like common sense to include your target market in the process, but remember, product designers and marketers have always thought in terms of age, not stage. Even if they included older adults in the design process, they include them *as older adults*, without any regard or respect for all the stages and nuances we've laid out here.

So you design a product or service for older people, and then the people in your market don't buy it and you wonder why. It's because they don't think of themselves as old. And even those that do think this way don't want a product for old people.

"Many product designers thought they understood the demands of the older market but underestimated how older consumers would flee any product giving off a whiff of oldness," notes Joe Coughlin, the founder and director of the AgeLab at MIT and one of the foremost scholars on designing for the older consumer.[6]

The gap between what multiple types of customers in multiple stages want and what companies design, create, and market to them is where the massive opportunity lies. A few best practices for those designing and marketing products for longevity have emerged.

Desirability Matters

The standard trope for designing for products for older adults is that they are "big, beige, and boring." This attitude in turn signals to people that it's an "old person's product," and if it's a consumer item, customers think it signals to the world that they use old people's stuff. But older adults in a learning stage or a renaissance stage, for example, are deeply interested in cool and fashionable purchases. They are interested in expressing themselves as individuals. And most crucially, they don't see themselves as a customer for old people's products, because they don't see themselves as old.

So, for example, OXO products are utensils for the kitchen and cooking. They also happen to be advantageous for people with arthritis, a common condition that many older adults, even active ones, will face. Most OXO items have large rubber handles, which are easy to grip. The company's line of kitchen utensils appeals to all types of cooks and is among the most desirable brands you will find in any kitchen.

Stealth Design for Marketing Wins

A key mistake in designing products for longevity is focusing on the features that are tailored to that demographic both in the design and in the marketing. Inevitably, no matter what stage someone is in, the physical and emotional changes associated with their age will play a role in good product design. Because many older people, for example, will face declines in visual clarity and color perception, small fonts on smartphone screens and low-contrast color schemes are challenging.

But that doesn't mean the customer wants to think about or even notice the features that help them overcome these limitations. Marketing should focus on the desirability and other features of an offering, not the fact that it includes some feature that's great for people with less dexterity.

A good example of this stealth approach is Nike's CruzrOne shoe, described in chapter 4. The company didn't focus on older runners but rather pursued lifelong athletes. The shoe included many features that served older people well—a sole that aided balance, provided extra cushioning, and more. But Nike didn't dwell on that or put it front and center before the customer, who would have, as Coughlin said, run the other way from an "old person's sneaker." Instead, Nike marketed a shoe that allowed people to do what they loved to do—run.[7]

If you are designing a user interface that requires less dexterity, or clothing that supports different body types, those features will serve your longevity customer well, but you don't need to sell that aspect. Better to focus on the elegant UX or the trendy colors and patterns of the outfit.

Multigenerational and Multistage Works

Even if you're designing a product for someone younger who is in an entirely different stage of life, you can design it with longevity in mind, especially if those features are stealth. For example, consider the user interface. Perhaps you simply design one for a younger demographic buying a particular car with a touch screen. But you use high-contrast colors and a large typeface that looks fresh and modern. It's trendy but also happens to appeal to a certain longevity customer who may need the larger type but wants to think about how cool and modern the touch screen looks.

You may also want people to perceive your products and services as naturally multigenerational in nature. Let's take a segment like workspace products and services. With a five-generation workforce, there are innumerable opportunities to reinvent furniture, meeting space, meeting tech, social networking, shared office space services, and much more to appeal to a multigenerational customer base, all of it sharing the same products and services.

You can also consider transitions between generations. Think about the younger customer who will move, for example, from the stage of providing financial security to an entrepreneurial stage. Which of this person's stage changes will obviate the needs for your products? And how will you retain this customer across that generational and stage shift? For example, a favored clothing line of exercise apparel might consider new sizing and easier closures for its older customer but would still have the same overall colors and styles. The clothing could also have additional features, such as zippers for people recovering from a hip replacement or knee surgery, integrating sensors, or pockets in biking clothing that are more easily accessible to hold phones and keys.

The Customer Is (Typically) Challenging to Acquire

Most businesses fail at targeting longevity because of their customer acquisition strategy. It is the single most challenging aspect of the longevity market. There are several reasons for this.

First, the acquisition costs tend to be higher than your traditional eighteen- to thirty-four demographic market. Part of this higher cost has to do with the adjacency in certain cases to health care; part of it is due to the previously discussed complexity between user, payer, and decision maker.

Second, identifying the best channel to target your customer is challenging depending on their stage and because you reach these customers using strategies different from traditional demographics. Direct mail, email, and Facebook work much better in this market than with others. Of all the major social media platforms, Facebook is still the main draw for older adults, much more so than Twitter and Instagram. Adults between fifty and seventy are quite responsive to Facebook advertising. Nearly 15 percent of users in this age range spend more than ten hours per week on the site. Of course, you still need to know their stage to effectively use the channel. Age segmentation simply lets you know where they are, not what message they want to hear.

In my own research and interviews with older adults, I have found that they prefer to hear about new products and services from a trusted resource as the informer. This observation is confirmed in the research literature.[8] Nike's ad for its CruzrOne athletic shoe for lifelong athletes featured Phil Knight, founder of the company and a fellow lifelong athlete. That is a trusted source. To increase vaccination rates during the pandemic, trusted members of different communities were deployed to promote the vaccine's safety and to share that they too had received one. Because these consumers are discerning and wary of being pigeonholed, trust is a major component of any marketing strategy to older adults.

Third and finally, many if not most companies dive into a direct-to-consumer model only to find out that a more nuanced strategy that involves business-to-business (B2B) and business-to-business-to-consumer (B2B2C) and sometimes public sector involvement is more successful. That was the situation for Honor, the home-care company profiled in chapter 4. Every time Honor entered a new geographic location, it needed to reinvent its go-to-market strategy. Direct customer acquisition required a knowledge of the local caregivers it could contract with and the complicated web of mom-and-pop operations in the market.

Even after the company gained local knowledge, the task of identifying individuals, one by one, to work directly for Honor was extremely labor-intensive. After years of marketing directly to those who provided care, Honor pivoted to form partnerships with home-care agencies and train the agency's professionals to operate under its own business model. This strategy sped the growth of the business but was a hard-won lesson.

The direct model was also challenging for Mon Ami, when in March 2020 the pandemic forced the company to reevaluate its business strategy of providing in-home respite care for caregivers.[9] Mon Ami was started in 2018 by two Stanford Graduate School of Business graduates. They hired college students to visit the homes of people aging in place and to engage in activities while the caregiver could take a much-needed break.

Initially, Mon Ami considered college students and family caregivers in its customer acquisition. When the pandemic hit, the model was threatened, obviously, but Mon Ami adapted. It canceled all in-person visits and established virtual visits for its existing customers. The company realized it could reach a much larger population this way and could add other services like delivery services for groceries and medicine. It added a meditation app, virtual exercise classes, and music performances.

Its quick scale-up in the pandemic got noticed, and a company that had only sold direct to consumers suddenly acquired a new kind of customer: the City of San Francisco. This big gain meant a new kind of customer relationship and marketing plan, but it also opened up further acquisition of customers through the city's own agencies serving families in need. Mon Ami now sells its technology support nationally to Area Agencies on Aging and other organizations that serve the needs of older adults. Time and again, I've seen longevity-focused companies pivot to a more complex customer acquisition strategy that usually involves both direct to consumer and business to business, and can often involves public entities.

The Customer Is (Definitely) Able to Spend

One of the strangest paradoxes of modern marketing is how the most money gets poured into inventing and selling products and services for a group that controls a proportionally smaller part of the spending.

People older than fifty account for more than half of all consumer spending in the United States and 83 percent of household wealth (with both numbers expected to rise). Internationally, McKinsey Global Institute has identified that the number of older adults will grow by more than 50 million from 164 million in 2015 and they will total about 222 million people in 2030. They will account for more than half of urban consumption growth, equivalent to more than $4 trillion.[10] Companies will have to prepare for this shift away from the long-assumed dominant demographics to the greater spending of longevity customers. According to McKinsey & Company, in a typical industry like consumer goods, companies only target customers in the nineteen-to-sixty age range (to say nothing of the different stages), ignoring and typically failing to understand the needs and nuances of longevity customers.[11]

To many companies, these customers are largely nonexistent. Monica, the renaissance stager at the beginning of this chapter, for example, has five times the net worth of a typical thirty-five-year-old. How can she and others feel so marginalized, so patronized by companies, if they represent such a big opportunity?

This is not to say that everyone in this market is wealthy. In fact, there are complicating factors to longevity, primarily in what it does to the financial profile of longevity customers. Nearly half of older adults would be living in poverty without social security, but because of that safety net, only 10 percent do.[12] With longer lifespans and healthspans comes more pressure on financial well-being. The majority of older adults will require innovative solutions to afford their longer lifespans and healthspans. A particular need involves innovations in housing to enable them to age at home.

The financial health of older adults is compounded by the shift from defined benefits to defined contributions in US pension systems. Because people have very different endowments, depending on how much they have saved, today's pension system has created a new form of inequality. But even here, companies in financial services should see opportunities to help older adults stretch their dollars and to better understand their options for decumulation. Companies looking to find older talent for mentorships or jobs also contribute to older people's financial well-being while also benefiting society by preventing increased poverty. Clever companies such as those pairing college students with older adults solve problems with loneliness and the cost of living for older adults and affordable housing for the younger.

The User Will Not Always Be the Payer

While I have just described the end user as the customer, there are three additional significant types of paying customers in the longevity market: employers, Medicare Advantage, and health plans who are not the end users.

Increasingly, employers are providing longevity and elder-care benefits to their employees, with one of the goals being to support the challenges that many employees face. Employers who offer more caregiving and longevity benefits do so as both a way to recruit and retain talent, and to increase employee wellness, productivity, and presenteeism. Companies such as Wellthy, Homethrive, Care.com, and CareLinx all provide care-coordination services for employees of their paying customers—the employer. Employers are also providing a wide range of health and wellness benefits, including wellness bonuses to support healthspan, funding for lifelong learning, and financial wellness. Expect to see an increase in longevity benefits that impact healthspan as well as lifespan, which will in turn create demand for new products and services under the umbrella of longevity benefits.

Another significant payer in the longevity market are Medicare Advantage plans. These are a type of Medicare health plan offered by a private company that contracts with Medicare to provide supplemental benefits, and are offered by a range of traditional health insurers such as United, Humana, and Cigna. These Medicare Advantage plans compete in the market for subscribers by offering new services and products. Over a third of all Medicare beneficiaries choose a Medicare Advantage plan, which often offers benefits such as membership in Wider Circle and Bold, as discussed in chapter 4.

The paying longevity customer is the individual Medicare Advantage Plan, while the end user is their subscriber. In 2018 and 2019, the Centers for Medicare and Medicaid Services expanded supplemental benefits that Medicare Advantage organizations can offer enrollees. This became a significant factor in the increased role of Medicare Advantage as one of the key payers, and hence a key customer for services and products. Moreover, beneficiaries must consider the value of these supplemental benefits when choosing a Medicare plan, adding to the complexity of the decision. This has led to new businesses being developed to serve those who need to choose which Medicare Advantage plan would be most advantageous to them.

Similarly, selling products and services directly to health plans that benefit their members has become a new type of longevity customer. Yet selling to these payers—employers and Medicare Advantage and health plans—has its own unique sales cycle (see chapter 6).

What Does Knowing the Customer Mean for My Business and My Employees?

You are now armed with the knowledge that longevity is creating new market opportunities and a range of customers. Longevity and older adults are not a liability but rather an economic driver. You also now know that customer acquisition can be more complicated in the longevity market, as is often the case for health-care products and services. The resulting channel challenge is the focus of the next chapter.

We need a more efficient marketplace in which to sell the range of products and services for multiple types of customers in various stages across thirty to forty years of life. Some organizations have made great progress in learning about and serving these customers, but there are huge missed opportunities for enterprising souls to come in and make significant impact while growing a business.

There is still groundwork to do, though. Purely demographic marketing and ageist strategies must be eliminated when companies are targeting the longevity customer.[13] As you are progressing here, your increasingly nuanced view of a complex market and vibrant dynamic customer base will help you overcome the ageism and blunt practices that have dominated until now but that are no long sufficient. This is important not just because it's good to treat older adults with dignity and respect and serve them in the ways they want, but also because you have no choice. This is where the market is moving. This is where growth will come from. Those who understand the customers get a competitive edge over those who don't.

RECOMMENDATIONS

- Remember that the longevity consumer is often misunderstood, partly because of the unique dynamics that are common in the health-care consumer markets. The purchaser may not be the end user.

- Recall that there can be as many as nine types of longevity consumers, and most categories are not the end user of the product or service.

- Consider who is making the purchasing decision. Target the daughter, daughter-in-law, other family member, or friend as well as the person needing care when you are creating products and services related to caregiving.

- Recognize the opportunities for a multigenerational customer base.

- Consider the customer acquisition challenges when choosing your marketing strategy.

- Design with, not for, the longevity end user. How can we ensure that older adults are at the center of the design of products and services?

- Mixed-age teams outperform those that are more homogeneous.

- Change ageist portrayals of older adults in your customer acquisition strategies.

CHAPTER 6

Tackling the Channel Challenges

For the longevity market to thrive, channels must be rethought. They are not efficient for the nature of this market. We need platforms and marketplaces that will support the inrush of startups, products, and services that will be invented for this swelling market. As author Daniel Pink says, "Remapped conditions require revamped navigation."[1] Not only do we need to solve channel inefficiencies and reimagine platforms and marketplaces for the longevity market, but doing so also creates opportunities in themselves.

Consider these older adults at different stages in their lives. They have something in common. Try to figure out what it is.

Tarun, seventy-two, is in his repurposing stage. He was making the transition out of his career but wanted to pay it forward by working with young people. He didn't teach in a school but wanted to share his knowledge about business with the next generation. He also wanted to pursue and share his woodworking hobby.

Mai, age forty-five, was in the stages of developing financial security and parenting; she was also in a caregiving stage because she was caring for her mother, who was in her legacy stage. One day, she took her mother to the hospital for a checkup and then home with an oxygen tank and some instructions on how to use it. Neither woman had used a tank before, and Mai was late getting home and driving her daughter to a birthday party.

Don, at eighty, was in his transition and repurposing stages. He had recently been widowed and now lived alone and needed to reconsider where to live, with his children far away. As a former physician, he also missed the practice of medicine and wanted to be involved in meaningful activities if he were to move. He was in good health and needed a way to navigate these transitions but didn't know where to begin.

Three people in the longevity market, three different situations, but all with a common challenge: none has easy access to what they need to be successful. Tarun had no idea how to match his desire to mentor or teach to younger people who could benefit either in business or woodworking. Mai could probably get the oxygen tank up and running, but she wasn't confident: What if she did it wrong? And what happened when the tank ran out? She had no sense of what to do, and she felt the pressure of other obligations as well. Don had many capabilities but needed to reconsider his housing situation and figure out how to repurpose his life and didn't want to be a burden to his children.

To be clear, what each of these people needed existed. There are platforms for matching mentors to younger people who have similar interests. There are geriatric care managers who can educate and assist people in complex caregiving tasks. And there are companies that provide coaches and resources for older adults who engage with transitions, purposeful activities, and housing platforms to assess alternative housing opportunities in different communities.

But the longevity market, for all its growth and promise, has not yet matured to expose these products to the customers or to deliver them efficiently. The market is a bit ragged at the moment. Word of mouth is too often the way people have found out about products and services. Advertising on social media platforms has become a newer conduit. Social workers in hospitals can be another source. Community groups another. But none is coordinated.

Finding the products and services is difficult for the customers and often requires long search sessions, diligent research skills, and a lot of time. Where do you find transition planning services as you move from one life stage to the next? Where do you find the range of financial planning services to support new stages? Where do you find the vast array of products and services for elder and parent care? How does a company that wants to sell longevity products to businesses even get started?

The information journey that customers must embark on is rarely efficient, nor does it provide direct connections to the solutions, products, or services the customer may benefit from and the companies want to sell. For example, an article in the *Wall Street Journal*, "How to Care for Aging Parents When You Can't Be There," contains a great list of resources that you could research.[2] However, every family would then need to conduct a detailed research project to find the resources that could aid their loved one or the caregiver.

Imagine thousands of people, all with different wants and needs, being unleashed in a giant flea market with no way to find what they're looking for except by wandering around, asking questions, and figuring out how to navigate the place themselves. The number of people who end up connecting with a seller will be far smaller than it could be, because the channel is so inefficient. A map of the market grounds would help. Targeted advertising in advance of the flea market would help. Professional shoppers. Whatever. Navigational links like these are often missing in longevity markets.

What is missing is the ability to integrate a search with the person's needs; a navigator to help identify the needs in light of specific conditions or life stage; the companies, products, and services that would be of assistance matched to their location; and then a referral to the company. These missing elements are achievable in the era of AI and machine learning. And they are affordable, if every company on the platform could solve its customer acquisition challenges and long sales cycles.

To date, there is no one-stop shopping platform for the services and products, so selling to the varied longevity customers is challenging.

Internet searches are the predominant method for finding products and services by consumers, but not in a specifically organized way. It takes effort and research skills to uncover the types of services and products that you may need or benefit from. The channel barriers are real. Every company has to determine if it will sell direct to consumers and which consumer platforms to use; whether to sell to employers as a benefit offered; and whether to sell to health-care plans, Medicare Advantage plans, Medicare, Medicaid, state or local government agencies, financial institutions, or some combination.

To illustrate the complexity of the channel challenges faced by companies, we can look at just a single domain—caregiving for older adults—and examine the range of channels that companies use to focus on solutions. In March 2021, I convened a roundtable of caregiving CEOs in partnership with Pivotal Ventures and the Aging2.0 Collective. Fifteen companies participated to share the pain points in their innovation journey and brainstorm solutions.[3] Among the most common barriers and challenges they face are these:

- Distribution channels: Companies are missing direct-to-consumer channels and encounter fragmented health channels.

- Systems design: The family caregivers are often not part of the professional caregiving teams.

- Misaligned incentives: The health-care system benefits from unpaid caregivers. And most of the $3.7 trillion health-care industry involves sick care and not health care.

- Market awareness: It's difficult to access insights and data about the customer or even identify who the customer is.

The work at the roundtable was eye-opening. In one exercise, we charted *nine* distribution channels the fifteen companies were employing, in many combinations. The channels were complex for us to chart; they must seem even more complex for customers looking for the right product or service. As one CEO said, "Even if you had a platform that enhanced access to family caregivers, by the time I speak with the sister, then the brother, then the caregiver, I have lost money!"

The market must be made more efficient. The solutions are valuable only if people can access them and only if companies can make a go of it providing them. Plenty of other markets are deeply systematic, coordinated, and efficient. A company like Wayfair, for example, doesn't have to worry about missing customers or having acquisitions costs soar because it takes so much to find and acquire its customers for furniture. That market is deeply interconnected and efficient.

The fact that various longevity opportunities face deeper channel challenges is something for marketers to keep in mind, of course. But these challenges also represent one of the greatest opportunities to create a two-sided marketplace that makes sense of the giant flea market for other companies.

Three key areas are ripe for further development: consumer channels, social and platform channels, and innovator and entrepreneurial channels. Here's a review of what exists in those channels now and where the opportunities are.

Consumer Channels

If you want furniture, you can go to one place to find many kinds: Wayfair, for example. If you want movies and TV shows, you have multiple subscription options to choose from: Netflix, Hulu, and so on. But there is currently no integrated digital platform for all the products and services that you may want to market to the longevity customer. And because of that, there's little data analysis you can do, because longevity customers aren't going to places where data could be collected to better serve them. An Amazon search may bring you initially to an array of books on aging in place, and a more diligent search could bring you to home-care products such as Alexa Care Hub, but interest in those products suggests other needs, such as addressing social isolation, transition planning, or repurposing for a new stage.

And those products are neither connected to nor easy to discover from the products you did find.

Companies trying to meet the channel challenge are doing it through a scaling-up strategy whereby they start in a narrow domain or subdomain such as Papa, discussed in chapter 4. Success in acquiring customers in one domain then helps them connect the dots to what else the customer might need, and the companies then expand to consumer-facing platforms and include a broader range of information and services.

Most of these scale-ups are in the caregiving and aging-in-place domains and subdomains. Best Buy, for example, opened a longevity consumer channel when it acquired GreatCall in 2018 for more than $800 million.[4] GreatCall made mobile phones and wearable devices that provide easy, one-touch access for the user to connect with family caregivers, obtain concierge services, or request emergency personnel. The company has since expanded, and under the name Lively, offers a variety of innovative, connected health and safety services, including daily medication monitoring, more connected products, and even information resources. Moreover, what started as a basic alert system for emergency communication has become a broader platform for aging in place at Best Buy Health with expansion into remote health services.

Similar stories are playing out with other platforms. For example, Seniorly offers an online platform to search for living arrangements for older adults both by location and by situation needed—respite care, assisted living, memory care, and independent living, to name a few. It too has added informational resources for the most common questions and pain points, educational resources, concierge services, and more. A Place for Mom has similarly scaled. Cake, described in chapter 4, is another domain-specific platform scaling up to provide for all end-of-life care needs.

It's natural that caregiving and health-related areas would develop broader platforms first, because they are the more developed, better-understood part of the longevity market. But even these areas still lack a fully realized two-way consumer channel. Mai, who as described earlier brought her mother home with an oxygen tank, could benefit from better channels. Her need to set up the equipment correctly, know when and how to replace it, and make sure her mother is safe could be aided by a care navigator. But she would have to know about care navigators and how and where to find them. Care navigation is still a fragmented, local network that's not well integrated with informational resources related to her challenges, not just with the oxygen tank but with all the other products and services her mother needs.

Moreover, some systemic roadblocks, particularly those associated with the fragmented health-care system and the varied elder-care ecosystem, add to the channel challenge. The right channel depends on the complexity of the product and the target user. Developing reseller partnerships can extend your company's reach, service configurations, geographic areas, and technology support services.

Two of the most common channels currently for longevity products and services are Medicare Advantage plans and employer benefit programs. The long sales cycle for each of these types of channels and payers is a factor for all companies. Typically, the process of selling to a Medicare Advantage plan begins in January of the year that a plan may choose to offer your service or product, as the enrollment period is between October and December of that year. Similarly, selling to an employer can often require having an internal champion to expedite the process, and your ability to demonstrate the value of your product or service for their employees. The possibility of someday having a two-sided marketplace for longevity products and services could be a new channel to address these challenges.

Many more opportunities to become a full-service marketplace for longevity consumers remain, especially beyond the areas of caregiving and end-of-life services. But what about the burgeoning markets for people living longer healthspans and not yet thinking about assisted living or caregiving? People like Tarun, who is squarely focused on teaching and mentoring and pursuing his hobby. A few platforms have come along to try to help, but none has yet taken hold. For Tarun to find the products and services he needs, and for the companies to find him as a consumer, is still a struggle.

There is an opportunity in many of the domains and subdomains to integrate the consumer channel, but I believe there is a bigger opportunity to integrate *across several domains*. For example, imagine a platform that helps you plan for all the many components of healthy aging from ages sixty to beyond one hundred. More importantly, imagine the many stages that you may go through: continuous learner, repurposing, transitioning, working, starting a new company, becoming digitally literate each year, finding different communities to engage with, writing your memoirs, developing your legacy. There are some terrific companies and organizations that do each of these, but the vast majority of older adults don't know about them and would struggle to find them, and the vast majority of companies don't know how to find these potential customers.

The goal of integration is to help customers find what they're looking for by giving them more of what they need, smartly packaged in a single place. It's an opportunity for navigation at all levels. You're giving the customer the map to their longevity needs.

Social Media, Community-Based Channels

Social media is growing and will continue to grow as a powerful force in the longevity market. Far from being technophobic luddites, older adults in all stages are some of the most voracious users of social platforms. The ability of some companies to create community around longevity—both as a specialty platform devoted to certain stages and as a more general platform with parts of it devoted to longevity—will go a long way to improving the channel challenges that companies face in acquiring longevity customers.

Those platforms often start as a way to connect people—which as we've seen in previous chapters is itself a service for this market, especially for people aging in place and those in the renaissance stage looking for new groups to join. But these platforms will grow to become information repositories and product marketplaces as well. They can also become new avenues for both marketing and distribution for your business.

We all know about Facebook and the gigantic base of older adults that use it, but the social media and community landscape is much more nuanced and varied than that one platform. For example, you may not know about NORCs—naturally occurring retirement communities—but they are real and a real opportunity.[5] NORCs are buildings or neighborhoods with a substantial number of older adults. It is not a planned community but has simply happened over time. These communities are becoming more common as more people stay in their homes into the longevity years. Many NORCs, administered by nonprofit agencies that aid them in being more independent, address the problem of social isolation. Services may include food delivery, preventive health measures, social activities, and transportation, to name a few, and companies looking at NORCs are targeting a whole community—an existing, organic social network—rather than a customer here or there.

Blue zones are another phenomenon to look at. Researcher Dan Buettner has identified regions or cities where people live much longer than average and calls them blue zones. The term has taken on a life of its own in consumer marketing. So-called blue-zone products ranging from food to skin care and more are now featured in stores as offerings to help you live a longer lifespan and healthspan. The Blue Zones organization serves as an informal distribution platform for consumer goods.[6]

In Hawaii, the Blue Zones Project is a community-wide well-being improvement initiative that helps make healthy choices easier for everyone in Hawaii. Its strategy is based on this premise: when an entire community participates, the small changes contribute benefits to all: lowered health-care costs, improved productivity, and a higher quality of life. While many health initiatives focus on diet and exercise programs, this project focuses on comprehensively changing a community's environment so that individuals are nudged into making healthy choices. The project takes a systematic approach to improving well-being through policy, building design, and social networks—a true channel mentality.

Increasingly, municipalities are integrating community and social platforms in a continuum that is good for public health. Collaboratives in cities and such states as Massachusetts and New York are being set up to encourage active aging.[7] The World Health Organization defines active aging as "the process of optimizing opportunities for health, participation, and security in order to enhance quality of life as people age."[8] As discussed in chapter 5, Mon Ami now provides tech support and software to assist the types of agencies that are part of these collaboratives.

Managed care organizations are getting into the social platform business and are becoming an often-overlooked new channel for product and service recommendations. These providers have the financial incentives to integrate preventive care as a cornerstone of their delivery model. Certain integrated health-care systems, such as Kaiser Permanente, have made available to their members some extensive resources, including information on discounted nonmedical products and services, alternative living arrangements, staying independent at home, caregiving, common aging concerns from A to Z, and medication management, to name a few.

Similarly, the Mayo Clinic has created a new platform intended to deliver comprehensive and complex care to patients at home via a new technology platform that will also include ways to ensure access to the patient's services and product needs.[9] This consumer-centered model can also become a distribution channel.

. . .

All these community-based, social media channels or consumer channels provide access to information, but most consumers still do not know about them. We need to do better at accelerating access to them, and in so doing, we would provide a new channel for the distribution of information, products, and services. Imagine that each of these channels could be linked to each of the eighteen stages you or your customer is in. In the same way you can go to find a variety of gifts for a wedding through Zola, you could now find a variety of products and services to support your stage.

Channels for Innovators and Entrepreneurs

As an innovator, you may look at databases such as those provided by PitchBook, Crunchbase, and CB Insights to find information about startups. There, you may find some information about ventures in the caregiving, home-care, and aging sectors, for a few stages. And those entrepreneurs need better ways to connect with their potential customers. A search for "longevity companies" in those databases will often bring you to startups that are developing biologics and precision medical therapeutics to extend life.

You'll find much less information about the dynamic and growing number of opportunities in the more broadly defined longevity market with all eighteen stages, a market that includes people who don't even think they're old! All the opportunities I've been talking about throughout this book—leisure and travel, second careers, learning, community building—need a bigger presence in the entrepreneurial ecosystem.

Several newer platforms are emerging for different components of innovation in the longevity market. A few new emerging collaboratives and accelerators can become a form of an innovation channel and could be extended to the longevity customer over time. Netflix solved the channel challenge for film, Wayfair solved this for furniture, and we need to solve this for healthy aging and longevity.

For example, the Hatchery innovation lab was launched by AARP to help develop products and services for any longevity customer. If the Hatchery chooses to buy or invest in a company, the lab can also help distribute the newly acquired products or services, complete with the AARP seal of approval. The Hatchery's goal is to support the entrepreneurship community and create bold services, products, and solutions for people fifty-plus. It also sponsors Silicon Valley–like innovation challenges and live pitch events with financial prizes. The innovation lab has partnered with other accelerators and, more recently, launched the AgeTech Collaborative to invest in and support the development of companies focused on longevity and to connect them with test-bed organizations to pilot innovations.

The Aging2.0 Collective is another initiative created to activate and nurture innovation in aging around the world. It includes more than eight years of data on innovations spanning more than eighty countries. Two thousand-plus companies occupy the platform. The Collective's database relies on 120 ambassadors who help foster matches in specific geographic locations. The Collective is intentionally an international platform, as it can provide new distribution networks for companies based in countries with smaller populations but with innovative systems for longevity and aging beyond what currently exists in the United States.

The AgeTech Accelerator, based in the United Kingdom, has identified more than a thousand companies that address thirty-six domains, including clothing, transportation, legacy, and learning in the longevity domains and the numerous aging care services and products.[10] The accelerator has grouped these companies into three categories:

- Serving areas that are mature, lack traction, or need consolidation

- Serving areas where development is currently focused

- Serving gaps in the market and future opportunities such as home diagnostics, sensory assistance, enhanced food and drink, mobility assistance, and robotics, and more

As mentioned earlier in chapter 4, a more recent entry is the new Techstars Future of Longevity Accelerator, formed in partnership with Pivotal Ventures in 2020. The accelerator focuses exclusively on developing solutions for caregivers of older adults and their recipients. Over the three-year accelerator program, Pivotal Ventures is also supporting several organizations and initiatives focused on enhancing solutions for and making the market more responsive to families' changing needs, as well as being part of a coalition of partners working to pass a comprehensive federal paid leave policy to support family caregivers.[11]

• • •

The creation of consumer platforms and social networks, coupled with the emerging innovation platforms, would create a more efficient marketplace for products and services; reduce customer acquisition costs, which are frequently a barrier for scaling and success; and, importantly, improve the lives of the millions of people as they live past one hundred.

Just as we have recommended using the preceding existing platforms to access end users, increasingly we may see community organizations such as the YMCA and YWCA as platforms through which companies can distribute services and products to their members both virtually and in person. Because certain community organizations such as the Ys serve a multigenerational community, some offerings that could benefit multiple generations could be channeled through such partnerships.

Still, even with all this emerging progress, there is no one-stop shopping or distribution channel for the entire range of longevity and healthy aging products and services. Thus, integrating platforms is one of my top recommendations (found in chapter 7) for finding opportunity in the longevity market: that these different existing platforms—consumer, social media, and community-based platforms—be integrated and made accessible to the actual longevity customer. Such integration will both enhance distribution and solve the channel challenge for companies and provide access to services and products. To be sure, some federal and state policies and public-private partnerships will also enhance access to needed solutions to support healthy aging, and these are addressed in chapters 7 and 8.

An International Perspective

Interestingly, channels are more well developed in countries that have a greater financial stake in the social and health-care services and systems they provide to their populations. If you're looking for inspiration, look to the countries with sophisticated channels that don't face the same customer acquisition or distribution challenges the fractious US system does.

England, Denmark, Singapore, Israel, and Canada are just a few of the countries that have created more efficient marketplaces and distribution channels and that are now creating comprehensive longevity systems—and not just for the caregiving slice of longevity. These countries are addressing the varied needs of healthy aging and longevity through national efforts for digital literacy programs and expanded education and work opportunities for older adults, that are in part sponsored and supported through their government agencies.

Denmark is often viewed as the premier model to emulate. When asked about what inspired Israel's comprehensive approach to the longevity market, Yossi Heymann, CEO of the Joint Distribution Committee-Eshel, the association for planning and developing services for older adults in Israel, responded, "We went to Denmark!" He promptly explained that a report on an Israeli delegation's visit to the Forum for Wisdom conference (Copenhagen, Denmark, July 2018) cited "the Danish model" for employment and pensions, and the resulting recommendations from an organization called Think Tank: The New 3rd Age, which is part of the Danish pension company PFA.

The Danish think tank focused on health, the transition from work-life to retirement, and housing as three central themes. It embraced the concept of a multistage life and a rewiring of the old three-stage model of careers (education, work, retirement). The thirty-three recommendations outlined in the PFA think tank's report "The Good Life in the 3rd Age" are now being embraced in places like Israel.[12] Among the most noteworthy are these:

- Investment in entrepreneurship

- Personal commitment to lifelong learning

- Educational savings for a change of career

- Partnerships to develop innovative platform-economic models

- Technology to support health in one's own home

- Better opportunities to engage in voluntary work

All these are business and innovation opportunities. And the better integrated the channels, the bigger the opportunity.

● RECOMMENDATIONS

- Look for varied consumer platforms to distribute your products and services.

- Use social media and webinars to reach older consumers and their influencers, such as their children.

- Understand the long sales cycles when dealing with employers, Medicare Advantage, and insurers.

- Consider creating new platforms for the consumer of your products or services.

- Remember the customer acquisition challenges when developing your strategy.

- Utilize the networks of the Village to Village Network (see chapter 4), Area Agencies on Aging (chapter 5), various healthy aging collaboratives, and other current platforms to reach your longevity customers.

CHAPTER 7

The Entrepreneur's Opportunities

Venture capital and entrepreneurship has long skewed young. Young investors target young innovators with young companies that have ideas for products that serve, for the most part, young people. But the money and talent in the venture capital ecosystem has a huge opportunity in the surging longevity economy. Already, some venture capital is flowing toward this market and industry heavyweights are getting involved, shifting dollars to support ideas that support older adults' wants and needs. The entrepreneurial ecosystem will also benefit from supporting and fostering older adults in a new stage of their lives. These people want to be entrepreneurs, so-called olderpreneurs, and bring deep experience and a new energy to driving innovative ideas for longevity.

Alan Patricof is a legend in the venture capital world. From his earliest investment in *New York* magazine to the founding of his own private equity firm Apax Partners and to the more recent founding of venture capital firm Greycroft Partners, Patricof has been part of the development of major companies like America Online, Office Depot, Apple, and Audible.

So when Patricof makes investment moves and talks about them, people pay attention, as they did when he challenged common notions that are changing in the venture capital and startup communities: "It's our responsibility and opportunity to build and invest in products, services and technologies for older adults—a sector that has long been ignored by venture capital money. In addition, the older adults we invest in have invaluable knowledge and experiences that can't be overlooked, and they're bringing brilliant ideas to the table. At age 85, I want to be the spokesperson for what's possible and drive society forward."[1]

That's what Patricof said when, in 2020, he partnered with Abby Miller Levy, then age forty-five, former president of Thrive Global and former senior vice president of strategy at SoulCycle, to create Prime-time Partners, a venture capital fund that will invest in startups catering to older adults. The duo raised $32 million during the pandemic. Their aim is no less than to defy the myth that older adults aren't online, don't buy things, and don't change their behaviors. Patricof and Levy believe that this group does, and will, do these things.

They are right. As encouraging as the announcement of the new fund was, something else was equally promising and newsworthy. Patricof, a seasoned and successful venture capitalist, recognized the enormity of the opportunity, but he was also going to be an active partner and founder at age eighty-five. Part of Primetime's investment thesis is to support older entrepreneurs.

Longevity Venture Capital Gains Momentum

Primetime has outlined a portfolio strategy with seed and early-stage investments in products, services, technologies, and experiences for aging in place, financial security for retirees, care management, longevity health services, and enriching consumer experiences. Investing in older adults who form new companies to capitalize on their experience is an important and novel approach in a venture fund. Patricof and

Levy are also backing Carewell, a company and platform that delivers health-care supplies, meal replacements, and education on home care for caregiving stagers.

The entrepreneurship opportunity extends to all innovators regardless of age, of course, but will obviously benefit from team members who understand the older adult perspective and needs. It will also benefit from someone who brings the stage, not age, point of view. "Design with, not for" is the standard mantra for developing innovations for older adults. As noted earlier, big, beige, and boring is out.[2] Stealth design that is attractive to intergenerational longevity customers is in. Fifty to sixty years old is not the end; it's a new beginning. The importance of including an older and experienced entrepreneur on the team is supported by research. By 2019, more than 25 percent of new entrepreneurs were between fifty-five and sixty-four—up from about 15 percent in 1996. By 2020, people fifty-five or older owned 43 percent of the country's small businesses.[3]

As explained earlier in the book, I use the increasingly common term *olderpreneurs* to describe this growing klatch of founders and innovators, and many others do, too. It's not the most elegant term; it has had mixed reviews. But it does capture one of the concepts that Primetime Partners is addressing, and it helps defy the stereotype belief that founders are mostly under thirty and that venture partners aren't "retirement age." Many are, and that's both good and valuable to the investment.

Increasingly, venture capitalists both within companies and at independent funds are recognizing this enormous investment opportunity. Most of the leading firms are investing in this space; they include Andreesen Horowitz (also called a16z), Blue Venture Fund, Khosla Ventures, Maverick Ventures, Oak HC/FT, and GoAhead Ventures. With Patricof's and Miller Levy's Primetime Partners have come a bevy of specialized funds for longevity opportunities, such as Generator Ventures, Magnify Ventures, Portfolia, Springbank Collective, and 7wireVentures. Specialized funds also exist in specific stages and domains within the market, for example, for senior housing. These firms form affiliations with senior living communities, where they have built-in beta sites to test products and services. Both Brookdale Senior Living and Hebrew Senior Life in the Boston area provide opportunities for research on products and services to benefit older adults. (Examples of many of the known venture firms investing in the longevity and healthy aging opportunity are included in the appendix.)

But as discussed, the opportunities are much broader than for those who reside in senior living. There is an enormous need to design products and services for the more than 90 percent who will age in place and the many transitions that will occur in the eighteen stages of life under the five-quarter umbrella. Importantly, we need new financial products that enable financial wellness to support longer lives.

The longevity market may also upend some other venture capital conventional wisdom. Typically, funds search for unicorns—the company that can reach a billion-dollar valuation. This market, however, seems to swap out the burning desire for unicorns for an impact investing model of good market rate of returns *plus* enormous societal impact. In the years ahead, impact investors will likely be engaging in these opportunities, much like the Emerson Collective's investments in Tembo Health, GoodTrust, and Free Will, as well as Innovations for Impact Fund's investment in Amava and MemoryWell, and Rethink Impact's investment in Wellthy.

Still, many venture funds do not yet have an investment thesis around longevity, and too few have made a commitment to develop one. It is another tremendous miss, as this opportunity is one of the biggest in history, one that my colleague Rob Chess, lecturer at the Stanford Graduate School of Business, likens to the software boom in the 1980s and the internet in the 1990s. "I think this opportunity is bigger, and more certain, given the demographic trends," Chess says. "Everyone is going to wish they had invested in this."[4]

The amount of capital available for venture investment has grown dramatically over the past four decades, yet only in the last five years has growth come to the older adult market, and much of that new investment came in the predictable, mature markets of elder care and home health care, where investment exceeded $1.1 billion in 2020.[5] But the venture capital community is still slow to understand stage, not age; longer healthspans; and the implications of these approaches.

Established venture funds explaining why they have not yet invested in this space mention three issues that have caused them to be late to the opportunity. First, many investors still think demographically. If you say *longevity*, they think about senior facilities, fall prevention, and traditional elder-care needs. They may have an ageist point of view on the opportunity. They think narrowly about "old people." Even those that may understand the demographic fact of an aging population haven't taken the time to understand the implications of increased healthspan and the many stages that older adults may experience. And if they haven't thought about that, chances are slimmer that they've developed the sophisticated understanding that readers of this book have on the intergenerational nature of the market and the nuances of users, payers, and providers. In short, they haven't put the time in.

Second, as mentioned, venture capital firms typically look for unicorns. The longevity market often maps more closely to impact investing in which social good takes precedence over economic returns, rather than the more traditional practice of searching for at least one big hit among many higher-risk bets. Even so, at least two longevity startups, Honor and Papa Health, have reached unicorn status with a valuation over $1 billion, and may be indicative of a new investment appetite.

Third, investors can't point to many successful exits—venture capital jargon for investments that turn a healthy profit either through getting acquired or going public. Most firms could point to maybe four that they know about, like Best Buy's 2018 acquisition of GreatCall for $800 million in cash, IAC's 2019 acquisition of Care.com for $500 million (after a prior initial public offering in 2014), Tivity Health's purchase of SilverSneakers in 2006, and Amazon's 2018 acquisition of PillPack for $753 million (see table A-4 in the appendix). In a business built on risk management, that's not a great track record. The scarcity of successful exits provides plenty of metric evidence that funds *shouldn't* make investments in longevity. Of course, this conclusion is a classic Catch-22: to invest, firms want to see successful exits, but to see successful exits, they have to invest. The only way past this dilemma is for some firms to go in bold, regardless of past performance. These bold moves are starting to happen. Expect those companies to be rewarded for getting there first.

Given the range of opportunity and the spectrum of needs beyond the traditional elder-care markets, we should see a far more substantial investment in the many domains, subdomains, and stages of the consumers identified in this book, and some that may not yet be on the radar of most investors and entrepreneurs. Expect some of the major investment conferences, such as the annual J.P. Morgan health-care conference, to devote sessions dedicated to companies focusing on the longevity opportunity.

New Opportunities for Entrepreneurs

Opportunities exist across every stage in the longevity market in dozens of domains and subdomains. In caregiving alone, the range of needs and products to meet them fall into as many as twenty-six domains and subdomains. Smart investors, though, won't limit themselves to caregiving. The aging domain is only a slice of the longevity market, as I've outlined in previous chapters. Many of the longevity market opportunities are described in chapter 4. Here are several additional opportunities that may not yet be on the radar of most entrepreneurs and investors but that will become integral to the longevity market and the smart investors who put capital into it.

Digital Literacy and the Digital Divide

Despite sizable gains in the number of older adults who have access to broadband internet, the numbers are still lower than they are for other groups. In the United States, 42 percent of the over-sixty-five population, lack access. This at a time when more and more products and services will require access. Increasingly, digital access is and will become the primary delivery vector for such basic services as health care, food services, and entertainment. It's also a core tool to help reduce the loneliness that threatens those aging in place. Increased healthspans will require increased access to digital tools and increased digital literacy.

Most older people use tech, but few would consider themselves completely fluent in the newest technologies. But don't mistake that for a lack of willingness. Despite stereotypes, older adults are quite willing to learn new technology, especially technology that helps them live independently. Providing this access, and the ongoing learning to keep up with new tech, is a major opportunity for entrepreneurs.

The Covid-19 pandemic accelerated digital literacy with technologies like Zoom, which people relied on for connection to family, friends, doctors, and information, but raises the question: Why did it take a pandemic to accelerate this part of digital literacy? Enterprising inventors could have been driving this development before it was forced on people. Older adults proved adaptable but lacked support services to enhance their capabilities. Some new organizations, such as Senior Planet and OATS (Older Adult Technology Services), have seen this opportunity and provide technology instruction and support to older adults.

Some countries have national education programs to address gaps in digital access and literacy; in the United States, several excellent nonprofit organizations are working on this issue. Denmark and Israel have created nationwide sponsored initiatives to educate everyone over fifty in digital literacy not just once but multiple times to keep up with new technology and platforms. These countries understand that older adults right now cannot rely on their grandchildren to be the providers of that education. Only a few for-profit companies have emerged despite what will be enormous demand, but overall, for-profit investment in digital literacy is not widespread. More will need to emerge.

Navigators

In chapter 6, we looked at how the lack of integrated channels makes longevity opportunities complex and difficult to navigate. An entrepreneur who can make sense of that complexity and simplify it for the user, purchaser, and payer will win big. Think of a platform company like Coinbase. This company has nothing to do with the longevity market—it is a platform for understanding and participating in cryptocurrency markets.

Cryptocurrency is a notoriously complex technology, and the market for it is similarly Byzantine. For that reason, it had low levels of adoption, primarily with technically savvy people. Coinbase aimed to make cryptocurrency available to anyone by helping laypeople navigate the complexity with ease. It became a unicorn startup as a result.

The same opportunity exists in the longevity market. A platform probably doesn't have to do much more than provide the navigation aid to be successful, whether it's help in navigating caregiving, end-of-life services, or something else. Cake, a platform discussed in chapter 4, views itself as navigators of the complex end-of-life market. Companies are also emerging to help Medicare-eligible people and their family members choose the best plans. Navigators tend to offer two things that help them stand out—knowledge and concierge-like guidance from professionals.

Transition Planning

Given the many stages in the longevity market—I list eighteen, but you may define others, and new ones will emerge over time—we know that older adults will enjoy several stages throughout their last four decades. Moving from stage to stage requires planning. Entrepreneurs can build companies to help ease these transitions. Some companies, such as Amava, iRelaunch, ReBoot Accel, and Know Your Value, to name a few, have done just that. AI could play an important role in these companies as a way to identify likely paths through stages, to help people identify their next stage options, and to match them to location, needs, talents, and learning and upskilling resources. Related to this will be workforce reentry innovations—which can be sold to companies, not just individuals—and services that help people redefine their purpose and priorities at different stages in their longer lives.

Another interesting aspect of opportunities in transition planning is a strategy that targets people and organizations at non-longevity stages, i.e., during Q1 and Q2. Companies can help people and organizations plan for a future without retirement and for a more complex path after the financial security stage. Another opportunity lies in helping high school students, college students, and young professionals begin designing and mapping their own lives through the longevity lens of a multistage life course.

AI-Based Tools

No doubt AI will be woven through many innovations across domains, so much so that simply providing AI services for companies developing other longevity products is probably a viable strategy. The entrepreneur who, for example, can build AI models that use geographic, demographic, and sensor data to model location-specific customer demand may be able to market that technology to multiple companies targeting longevity customers. AI is already being used, unsurprisingly, in the health-care segment for people in their legacy or end-of-life stage. The technology helps identify who may not have an advanced directive when they are hospitalized, and other algorithms predict who is likely to fall. There are countless untapped ways that AI can be integrated into new products and services.

Loneliness, Isolation, and Redefining Purpose

Identifying ways to improve social connections and meaningful engagement throughout the different stages of aging and longevity will become increasingly important when much of our lives are online or in remote work settings. Novel ways to connect people with security and privacy will be needed.

Travel, Leisure, and Entertainment

Two areas stand out as opportunities for entrepreneurs in these domains. The first area focuses on people in the stages that prevent them from easily traveling or enjoying activities they would normally enjoy. This market may have gotten a bump from the pandemic, which forced many companies to reconsider what travel and entertainment can be. For example, Rendever sells virtual reality to assisted living communities so that groups of residents can gather to "visit" faraway places and museums together, sharing a simultaneous experience with others. In some cases, they can visit their hometowns with their grandchildren. Not only can such innovations bring joy, but they also help reduce isolation and loneliness.

The second prominent area is the multigenerational opportunity arising from older adults who are still in active stages, reimagining their lives, continuing to travel, and go to concerts and so forth. Intergenerational travel with multiple generations traveling together will increase with increased healthspans. Educational travel experiences for those in the renaissance stage will grow in demand.

Fashion and Accessories

There will be plenty of science to incorporate into this domain—clothes can be designed for longevity customers, and wearables can be engineered and programmed to their specific needs. This domain is a prime area for entrepreneurs to think like Nike—they are not serving "old people." Features can be delivered in stealth mode, as no older person wants to be marketed to with features that remind them of increasing limitations. Creativity is needed to enhance fashion with features that will facilitate different needs at different stages. For example, one focus could be on making stylish clothes, which also just happen to avoid buttons or zippers to increase easy on-off access. You can also expect technology to, literally, weave these areas together, as integrating monitoring devices into clothes looks like an important and open opportunity.

Fitness and Mobility

Although there are more than 250,000 health and wellness apps, few focus on older adults in good healthspan stages. There are several important trends in fitness and mobility services that enhance well-being. Focusing on the needs of those with more limited mobility will add to healthy aging and longer healthspans. Companies that can increase healthspans are effectively extending the length of time they can engage with their customer. Again, science will be active here, but also entrepreneurs should get past ageist notions of older adults and their relationship to tech around fitness and mobility. Older adults are able and willing to learn and engage with new technology. The company that designs it well for its market will win.

Lifelong Learning

Continuing education isn't a new concept, and many platforms exist to support it: GSVLabs, General Assembly, Flatiron School, Coursera, and edX, to name a few. None takes a pure longevity lens to its products. Understanding the needs of a renaissance learner, for example, compared with a caregiving learner will help you make better products more suited to these customers. Other models of learning tailored to older adults are waiting to be invented. The returnship model connects employers to people in the portfolio, transition, and repurposing stages—companies that can broker successful connections will do well. Encore.org fellowships provide a similar service for stagers who want to engage with nonprofits. There is a need for more venues for and approaches to continuing education. Currently we think of learning as something that lasts about twenty-five years in our lives, most of it front-loaded. That model will break down because learning lasts forty or more years and is spread through multiple stages. More opportunities for experiential learning and upskilling will be necessary and represent a great investment and business strategy.

Mentoring and Intergenerational Workforces and Engagement

Among the most satisfying relationships are often those between mentors and mentees. And with the swelling numbers of people who have left their primary careers, many will want to become mentors. Opportunities will be pervasive in this marketplace, especially the chance to help companies use older adults to their best advantage as talent developers. In addition, reverse mentoring to help older adults make the transition to new stages and roles can be a major opportunity. Organizations that match services and training to enhance these important relationships will gain a lead in the marketplace.

Housing and Intergenerational Living

Nearly 90 percent of adults prefer to age in their own home but not all will be able to do so successfully or afford to do so. Several new ideas have emerged to address this challenge, including intergenerational living communities. More of such living arrangements will be needed, as they will address a multitude of needs, including social isolation, loneliness, and tech support. The redesign of homes to incorporate universal design principles that support aging will become an integral part of construction and housing.

Telehealth

A positive change during the pandemic was the widespread adoption of telehealth services. Remote health-care services went from minimal to nearly 90 percent of appointments during the pandemic. When Medicare began to reimburse for telehealth services as well, the move was a game changer. There will be a need for more specialized forms of telehealth services and for more comprehensive health-care solutions, including services for older adults. Integration with sensor technology will transform telehealth from onetime appointments to continuous monitoring. And such monitoring can be combined with AI to predict events and make care suggestions. One example is developing specialty telehealth services such as sports medicine for older athletes to help prevent or treat sport-related injuries.

Suffice to say, the enormous opportunities ahead in health care are based on the idea that the home will become the location where much primary care takes place. Home monitoring will become even more prevalent. Smart tools and technology with modifications for the older user will be important. Health coaches and social support will be new additions to the care team as well.

Food and Nutrition

Home delivery of meals and groceries will become increasingly essential for older adults as they enter different stages. Tailoring meal delivery to different dietary and nutritional needs of older adults, some with varied medical conditions, will grow as an opportunity. These companies will often work with, or be purchased by, transportation options such as Lyft and Uber.

Platforms, Platforms, Platforms

No one has yet created a comprehensive platform and database that can support the range of innovations and needs that longevity consumers can access. Several good platforms, such as Seniorly and A Place for Mom, are available for housing needs, and Cake provides a good platform for end-of-life care. But no platform currently includes the spectrum of companies, products, and services that a family member of an older adult, a Medicare Advantage plan, an employer, or the older adult themselves may want to purchase for their care.

There's also a demand for platforms for transition planning, continuous learning stages, and the stages described in the five-quarter paradigm to help a person navigate the new life course presented by longer lives. A call to action by experts in search functions and in creating platforms would be most welcome.

Whatever Else You Can Imagine

One of the beautiful parts of entrepreneurship and innovation is how they create unexpected opportunities. Who could have predicted that innovations like the smartphone and an app ecosystem would fundamentally transform the taxi business? The truth is, we don't yet know all the opportunities that will be created by an extra thirty or forty years of life and health. Entrepreneurs will imagine new possibilities. But it starts with overcoming ageist stereotypes, understanding the stage approach in defining the market, and building from there. This list of entrepreneurial opportunities is by no means exhaustive or definitive. It's just the beginning, and not the end.

A Bonanza for Innovators: Design Challenges, Accelerators, Resources

The longevity innovation and entrepreneurship ecosystem now includes a variety of annual design and innovation challenges that have emerged over the past five to ten years.

Entrepreneurs developing innovative products and services for the longevity market are benefiting from a new trend, as startup incubators focused on aging are emerging across the country. These accelerator programs often belong to venture capital firms, universities, or large corporations and offer a range of resources designed to stimulate creative ideas for solutions. They support diverse teams of engineers, scientists, providers, and caregivers and provide access to users. Many of these offer support to entrepreneurs by providing mentoring, lab and field testing, advice on markets, customer discovery, and access to funding and partners. The goal in these accelerator programs is to improve the quality of life for older adults and those who care for them. Design themes are often based on one or more of the needs and domains associated with longevity. You can find a list of such programs in the appendix in the Resources for Entrepreneurs section.

In addition to these opportunities, entrepreneurs entering this space will also benefit from becoming familiar with a variety of new longevity resources that curate the many research reports, news about startups, and discourse on trends. Because these curating organizations also offer webinars and conferences on a range of topics, you may find it helpful to get on their subscriber lists. Again, a full list can be found in the appendix in the Resources for Entrepreneurs section.

The course now being offered at the Stanford Graduate School of Business, "Longevity: Business Implications and Opportunities," examines the unique aspects of the longevity consumer and aims to create new cohorts of entrepreneurs who understand the range of innovation opportunities presented. The course also stimulates discussion about students' own lives and careers as they consider the new map of life. Encouraging the expansion of, and participation in, entrepreneur-in-residence programs within companies and venture firms to focus exclusively on longevity, will also accelerate development and growth.

Integrating Longevity Entrepreneurship within an Organization

Intrapreneurship within larger companies and organizations will be important as well. We see intrapreneurship happening both through product and service innovation in established businesses, as we saw for Merrill Lynch, Nike, and Warby Parker, and through startups of new enterprises for the business. A longevity entrepreneur can become an internal champion who recognizes the opportunity for change.

P&G Ventures, for example, utilizes a team within the company to help design and source new products and services for longevity. The team issues design challenges around longevity domains and various stages of its longevity customers, including women's health, enhanced sleep, cognitive health, and aging at home.

Other companies in various industries have similar efforts underway. For example, Amazon now has an Alexa venture group that focuses on health and wellness, a domain that is prime for innovation to support longevity customers. The company has recently announced that Alexa Together will help you care for your family remotely, replacing the Care Hub. Thinking in terms of stages will help focus those ventures. BMW was one of the earliest companies to recognize the value of the older customer. It designed features in its vehicles to serve those customers. What's more, BMW used both internal champions and a design team that included older adults to create and market its innovations. And Best Buy has their new employees participate in sensitivity training using virtual reality to understand visual impairment, to better understand and better serve the needs of their older customers, whom they refer to as Gen A.[6]

The double benefit of creating this effort is that these companies then position themselves to better understand their own workforce and their needs. Merrill Lynch, as noted in chapter 4, has integrated its new customer-facing longevity products into employee benefits as well. Driving the conversation about stages with employees as well as customers will enhance the creativity and impact of the products and services you create. Change the conversation from "retirees" or "elderly" to the "repurposed" "rejuvenation" stages of life.

While entrepreneurship and innovation will address many of these new needs and provide enormous business opportunities, some of the necessary solutions will require policy innovation. We need policies that create an ecosystem whereby older Americans are valued for their wisdom and other contributions to our society and workforce and are respected for their need to live with dignity through all stages of a long life. The next chapter highlights the impact that our new long-lived society can have.

● RECOMMENDATIONS

- Recognize that aging is not the problem—it is the opportunity.

- Embrace the new narratives around aging versus the simple concept of *old*.

- Remember that the older adult population is diverse and heterogeneous in its needs and wants—if you have seen one eighty-five-year-old, you have seen just one eighty-five-year-old.

- Align your longevity innovation and customer with the stage of life they are in—using a broad framework of the five quarters and eighteen life stages—which often are not sequential.

- Identify who the purchaser is and which distribution channels you will access.

- Think about how you sell trust. Trusted relationships will enable you to sell a range of services and products.

- Develop and market to multigenerational customers.

- Recognize that product features need to be stealth.

- Incorporate the positivity effect and trusted advocate in your marketing strategies.

CHAPTER 8

Longevity Dividends

The innovations you create for the longevity market, and the products and services you introduce, will help grow your business and will reach an underserved and growing customer base. But you can create impact beyond that. By entering the longevity market and embracing a mindset of stage, not age, you are uncovering great opportunities to address ageism in your company, among your workforce, and in your marketing strategies. You have the chance to support policies that value the caregivers who also work for you and to create new ways to help this demographic enjoy longer healthspans and age with dignity. These are among the many dividends of the new longevity.

By now you see the expansive opportunity before you in the longevity economy. There will be no industry, no product domain, no market that isn't somehow affected by the demographic facts before us. There will be more people over sixty than ever before, and many more of them will be living healthy, active lives with diverse wants and needs.

The opportunity to improve your bottom line is massive, but so is the opportunity to participate in creating lasting social change. The truth is, the market, public policy, and cultural attitudes all need to catch up to this inevitable shift more than they have. It starts with understanding the market, which is everything we've considered to this point in this book: Understand the concept of stage, not age. Appreciate the complexity and nuance of the customer, user, and payer dynamics. Anticipate and help remove channel roadblocks.

Among the many dividends of the new longevity are the social, economic, and health benefits.[1] But the policy and cultural attitudes will need to change as well if the longevity market is to thrive. There are four key areas for you to invest in that will reap longevity dividends: combating ageism, effecting policy, investing in dignity, and fostering intergenerational community.

Combating Ageism

Mistaken attitudes and negative perceptions about older adults and their capabilities prevent success in the longevity market. As long as ageist attitudes are found in your organization, you'll fail to see the opportunities in front of you and fail to properly execute. You'll lose to organizations that are more age-aware and that have worked hard to root out ageism. By not helping to combat an ageist culture, you're diminishing your talent pool and decreasing the likelihood of success in a complex market that will require partnerships and fresh ways of thinking about how to attack challenges.

But you're not ageist, you think. Well, by reading this book, you've started to combat any intrinsic ageism you may possess—and we all do have some level of ageism, because it is persistent and deeply embedded in our culture.

The change starts internally. Findings from an AARP survey confirm that ageism persists in the workplace and in the job market. A full 28 percent of fifty-five-plus workers suffer long-term unemployment, compared with 18 percent of workers aged sixteen to fifty-four. "The long-term unemployment disparity suggests that entrenched age-bias still exist too often in the workplace," the report states.[2] More data:

- More than nine in ten workers see age discrimination as somewhat or very common.

- Three out of five older workers report that they have seen or experienced age discrimination in the workplace; of those concerned about losing their job in the next year, one-third list age discrimination as either a major or minor reason.

- On the job hunt, 44 percent of older job applicants say they have been asked for age-related information from a potential employer.

- Only 3 percent of older workers report making a formal complaint of ageism to a supervisor, a human resource representative, another organization, or a government agency.

- And 59 percent strongly support strengthening age discrimination laws.

Findings like these are increasing, as is public awareness about ageism. Data is being collected and addressed by Mercer, Transamerica Institute, AARP, the Milken Institute Center for the Future of Aging, and the Sloan Research Network on Aging & Work at Boston College.[3] Milken president Paul Irving and others wrote a series of articles on the age of no retirement in *Harvard Business Review* in 2018, documenting the impact of the longevity phenomenon and the need for enlightenment about the value of the older worker.[4]

But much more needs to be done. If workplaces are generally ageist, how can they be expected to approach a market for that group of people? To succeed in the longevity market, businesses must be part of the movement toward diversity, equity, and inclusion, which includes age diversity and age inclusion.

Longevity experts like to call talent efforts "turning ageism into sageism." That is, firms should recognize, reward, and reap the deep value found in the life experiences and knowledge accumulated by older employees.

There are concrete ways to start. One is to take a longevity pledge. Pledges are becoming more common because they create a way to hold a company accountable for its public statement of support of some change. In this case, many such pledges regarding longevity have emerged.

Under the AARP Employer Pledge, for example, companies affirm the value of experienced workers and commit to developing diverse organizations: "We believe in equal opportunity for all workers, regardless of age, and the 50+ workers should have a level playing field in their ability to compete for and obtain jobs. Recognizing the value of experienced workers, we pledge to recruit across diverse age groups and to consider all applicants on an equal basis as we hire for positions within our organization."[5]

The statement would be empty words and a PR stunt if it stopped there, but it doesn't. The pledge requests employers take two actions within the first two years of signing, and anyone can check on companies to see if they've failed to fulfill their pledge. Among the actions that AARP requests companies take are these:

- Review job descriptions and recruiting materials to ensure they don't include qualifications or language that discourage experienced workers from applying.

- Incorporate in recruitment materials language that states that workers of all ages are encouraged to apply.

- Don't require date of birth or dates of graduation as part of the application process.

- Include age as an element in diversity and inclusion strategies.

AARP has also worked with other organizations like the World Economic Forum and the Organisation for Economic Co-operation and Development to address ageism in the same way that some organizations committed to increase diversity in their workplace.[6] The effort will engage nearly one hundred global employers with a combined revenue of more than $1 trillion and represents 2.2 million workers. AARP is building knowledge within those institutions and facilitating a knowledge exchange between the companies. Crucial to this work is an intergenerational focus on the value of the "5C skills"—curiosity, creativity, critical thinking, collaboration, and change management, as ones that cross generations. The steps being recommended are guidelines and pledges to affirm the value of experienced workers and an age-diverse workforce.

Another way to combat ageism is to reimagine the portrayal of older adults in the media. Anyone who enters the market will quickly discover how much more diverse this population is than it seems in media and advertising. The FrameWorks Institute, in collaboration with the leaders of aging organizations, has conducted extensive research on this topic.[7] It reports that, typically, only two types of older adults are shown in the media: frail, diseased, senile people at the end of their life and in need of constant and expensive care or fully active, healthy, and wholly independent people requiring no support.

These diametrically opposed and extreme representations belie the fact that older adults exist on a spectrum of wants, needs, and care. These portrayals also overlook that even healthy older adults could benefit from offerings that provide them some form of physical benefit. Typical images feed the public's already-problematic perceptions of aging and stereotypes about older adults. FrameWorks and others suggest that narrow media representations of aging pose substantial challenges to advocates seeking to build greater understanding of older adults' needs and design policies to address those needs.

Municipalities have been quicker to address this issue than companies have. In 2019, the City of San Francisco launched a Reframing Ageism campaign, an attempt to overcome stereotypes by highlighting the creativity, intelligence, and may other strengths that older people contribute to our workplace and communities.[8] This is an especially powerful effort in the tech-heavy Bay Area, where youth is worshipped in the entrepreneurial and high-tech communities. The city posted large photos of all types of older adults with the taglines "This is creativity," "This is intelligence," and more on billboards, on buses, and throughout the area.

Each of these efforts will enhance the positive contribution of older workers throughout their lifespan and help promote ageless workplaces and communities. Addressing ageism in marketing campaigns, in design, and within the workplace is critical to creating products and services that will be needed by the range of longevity customers. The opportunity for companies here is obvious—to redesign their media and advertising when they are addressing the longevity market, or even intergenerational markets, to create more diverse and accurate images of older adults.

Progress on ageism is happening slowly. Ashley Martin, a faculty member at the Stanford Graduate School of Business, has described ageism as the last acceptable *ism*.[9] Only recently is ageism really coming under scrutiny, and companies can be part of this sea change in their boardroom, their workforce, and their advertising and marketing campaigns.

Out of the awfulness of the pandemic may come a silver lining with regard to ageism. The Covid-19 crisis forced us to increasingly recognize and value experienced professionals—older adults—and the importance of the work they did to fight the virus and save lives. Anthony Fauci, a physician and the director of the National Institute of Allergy and Infectious Diseases, became the most trusted and relied-on resource for truth and information in the nation. Tens of thousands of retired health-care professionals came back to work to help combat the disease in hospitals. Programmers who knew obsolete programming languages became essential to salvaging government databases. *Experience*, *wisdom*, *essential*, *action*, and *trusted* emerged as the words connected to these older adults. Society perhaps began seeing older adults as assets again.

And if work becomes increasingly remote, age may recede as a primary factor in recruiting and retaining talent. If anything, the increased competition for talent as people can work for geographically distant employers will mean that companies will have to consider prospects of all ages if they are to compete. Working remotely may also inadvertently become a great equalizer, as more older workers become more fluent in the technology needed to be effective—technology an ageist culture believes older adults can't or don't want to embrace. All these developments could combine to shift company cultures. They will integrate longevity for their employees as well as for their products and services. Employers will increase the value placed not just on knowledge but also on wisdom.

Effecting Policy

In any shift as seismic, broad, and culturally all-encompassing as this longevity shift, policy tends to follow the change. Industrialization transformed labor and business policy; the introduction of broadcast media required a years-long revision of laws and regulations around content; and the internet, of course, has upended telecom policy multiple times. Likewise, the new longevity will see a similar reappraisal of any number of policies, including retirement, social security, health-care policy, and building codes. Companies will benefit by actively participating in the reformulation of policy, potentially accelerating some of the markets they want to enter. Those that don't will have to play by the rules others make.

How this policy is shaped may even determine whether a market for your product will exist because the payers for your products and services may be subsidized by the policy. In caregiving and health care especially, most people who need services will not be able to fully afford them.

Telehealth, for example, is not breakthrough technology; it has been available for years, but not until Medicare changed its reimbursement policies to fully cover virtual visits did telehealth became nearly universally accessible and affordable through game-changing policy in 2020. Think of the ecosystem around telehealth: the opportunities arising from communications and sensor technology, new concierge services, new caregiving models, new content and educational opportunities, capabilities to connect apps to medical records and billing systems—the list goes on and on, and none of it opens up if the policy isn't put in place.

Policies that will enable incentives to save for aging-related needs and services could make an impact on the lives of millions and create

a pathway for many businesses. Could we have "longevity bonds" similar to the notion of baby bonds to assist people with saving for longer
lives?[10] Will the assortment of products and services that could support
healthy aging and longer life be affordable for most individuals, or could
government incentives and support help reduce costly hospitalizations?
Some states, such as Washington, have implemented policies that will
ease the financial burdens associated with caregiving and aging and
provide tax credits to caregivers.

Other industrialized countries pay family members to be caregivers
(in the United States, this is only the case if the family is sufficiently
impoverished to qualify for Medicaid). Norway, Sweden, Japan, and
Germany are among those that provide health benefits to protect families from out-of-pocket expenses and serve as policy models for companies to consider and help implement in their markets.

The United States is starting to invest. As of this writing, the Biden
administration has put forth a $400 billion-plus initiative to address
many of the challenges of aging and longevity, including tax incentives
for retaining older workers and a $5,000 tax credit for family caregivers.
The administration is also proposing to offer social security credits for
people who care for a loved one and is strengthening programs such
as Capable (Community Aging in Place—Advancing Better Living for
Elders) to include home repairs and modifications. It is also proposing
to add 150,000 community health workers and a national strategy to
recruit, retain, and empower the caregiving workforce.

Other policy initiatives, such as paid family care leave and the Credit
for Caring Act introduced in May 2021, would provide up to $5,000
federal tax credit for eligible working family caregivers to help defray
the approximately $7,000 that many families spend each year in out-of-
pocket caring costs. These initiatives will be another recognition of the
value of the forty-eight million people who provide unpaid care to older
adults.

As shown in this short synopsis, companies that think in terms of
stage can see multiple opportunities in technology, finance, construction, and talent retention.

Melinda French Gates, who is active in thinking about longevity, has proposed the idea of a national caregiving czar to address the policies needed to support caregivers in the United States. This type of leadership and the recognition of the necessary support systems are essential for the innovation opportunities and challenges ahead for older adults and families. She has also supported the need for national paid leave, as she eloquently articulated in her recent article asserting that our economy is powered by caregivers.[11]

When talking about policy, we naturally gravitate toward health care and a few stages—transition, legacy, end of life. But policy will affect many other stages as well. Renaissance stagers intent on learning opportunities will benefit from reimagined education policy.

Financial companies designing longevity products may see changes in social security policy or tax policy as valuable to opening business for younger people who are nevertheless planning for later stages in life. These companies will create products to help people better understand how far their investment assets will last and ways to increase their value. They could also expand such services to include transition planning and ways that tax policies for continuous learning could support that.

Companies will ignore the policy implications of longevity at their peril. Many modern success stories about new businesses are built on a company's seizing on change, recognizing the policy implications, and effecting the change. Netflix's success, for example, is built on its being both a distributor and a producer of content, something that was once not allowed. But when the policy shifted, the opportunity opened up.

Investing in Dignity

In a market like longevity, the dignity of the customers matters. For legacy and end-of-life stagers, the ability to manage and control the process will be crucial. We must consider the question of who pays for older adults' care, including long-term health care. In the United States, since Medicare does not pay for most long-term care, middle-income older adults will be unable to afford all their fees if and when they need assistance.

Dignity also means creating a deeper focus on the role of caregiving in our culture, and it can't be achieved if ageism persists. The failure to inject dignity into the market will create bad outcomes and a public health crisis. Even now, stories of poor conditions in care facilities are too common. Poor wages and training for caregivers exacerbates the issue, creating poor outcomes for those facing the final part of their life.

Investing in dignity is not only a good thing to do but also a potential competitive advantage. Companies that support the caregiving community open new business opportunities for many stages, including the stages at which people want to plan for later life stages earlier in their lives.

But what does it mean to invest in dignity? In part, it will be to understand and participate in the formulation of new policies and plans with government support. For example, in Washington State, a new payroll assessment funds a novel program. A 0.58 percent tax on employee wages takes effect in January 2022 to fund long-term-care assistance. This program will help offset the needed savings to prepare for longer lives. Employees with long-term-care insurance are exempt. The trust program will provide long-term care for a lifetime maximum of $36,500 per person, and qualified family members acting as family caregivers are eligible to receive payments as well for their services.

Several other states have embarked on statewide initiatives that comprehensively evaluates the needs of their aging population. In early 2021, California released its Master Plan for Aging.[12] The five goals and targets outlined in the plan are useful guides for thinking about both challenges and opportunities:

- Housing for All Ages and Stages: We will live where we choose as we age in communities that are age-, disability-, and dementia-friendly and climate- and disaster-ready. Target: Create millions of new housing options for healthy aging.

- **Health Reimagined:** We will have access to the services we need to live at home in our communities and to optimize our health and quality of life. Target: Close the equity gap and increase life expectancy.

- **Inclusion and Equity, Not Isolation:** We will have lifelong opportunities for work, volunteering, engagement, and leadership and will be protected from isolation, discrimination, abuse, neglect, and exploitation. Target: Keep increasing life satisfaction as we age.

- **Caregiving That Works:** We will be prepared for and supported through the rewards and challenges of caring for aging loved ones. Target: One million high-quality caregiving jobs.

- **Affordable Aging:** We will have economic security for as long as we live. Target: Close the equity gap . . . and increase elder economic sufficiency.[13]

Each of these goals provides new opportunities for innovators and a partner in state government to help pay for these solutions. The goals also aim to address the inequity gap and to promote designing for affordability.

Innovation will be necessary and will open up even more opportunities. Leading economists and longevity thought leaders talk about several such innovations they believe can make a difference to dignified aging. Among their suggestions are these:

- Baby bonds to support long life

- Educational savings programs to support lifelong learning

- Financial incentives for companies that retain older workers

- Updated laws on mandatory retirement age

- A national service year for young adults between high school and college, in which they serve as support and companions for older adults

- National and state digital literacy and financial literacy campaigns for older adults

- A national service model addressing the aging sector in exchange for stipends and educational grants for college

- A permanent lifting of Medicare location restrictions on telehealth to ensure that older adults can receive a variety of services in their homes and communities, regardless of where they live

- Increased equitable access to telehealth services

- Income tax credit for caregivers to offset the cost of caregiving

- Increased compensation and salaries for paid caregivers

- National paid leave for caregiving to older adults

- Tax credits for learning sabbaticals

The Covid-19 pandemic has been a catalyst to reexamine just about every aspect of our lives and our economy: work, transportation, housing, health care, and social connections, for example. It has also brought some of the most important conversations about dignity and aging to the fore. Conversations about end-of-life care, death, and dying came to the kitchen tables and device screens of so many. While painful at times, these conversations are critical and have created a brighter focus on the role of dignity in this economy. Some of the innovations that were created during the pandemic, such as the respectful way stores created shopping hours for older adults, can be integrated permanently into our culture and will foster dignity. For example, new startups emerged to help provide food and tech support to the aging population and opened up telehealth to the masses in a way that will improve care for those who need it most.

Fostering Intergenerational Communities

Longevity customers don't exist in a vacuum. Increasingly, experts see the intergenerational realities in the workforce and the community as crucial to making sure older adults can thrive and live dignified lives. Those longevity experts have also shown that simply creating intergenerational connections pays dividends to *both* sides of that connection—both the older adults and the younger generations. We now know that intergenerational learning settings contribute to the learnings of both younger and older students. And organizations that provide new opportunities for intergenerational engagement help all generations thrive.

Multigenerational workforces, with as many as five generations in one workplace, will become more typical. I have outlined how these workforces will enhance collaboration and product design. The wisdom factor, the experience factor, and the collaboration factor will contribute to the success of companies. Reconfiguring the workplace to include reverse-mentoring opportunities will help companies thrive. Reimagining higher education to include older and younger students will help all students learn more. Mercer advocates that all companies become age-ready organizations by integrating policies to have a multigenerational workforce and providing data to support the increased value of multigenerational teams.

The changing idea of where people work is emerging as an intergenerational opportunity. Companies like Salesforce have moved to permanently allow a majority of their employees to work remotely at least several days a week. Others have followed. This practice will be a game changer for all and will open opportunities for older adults who wish to continue to work longer and companies that want to serve them with useful products and services (especially in learning and caregiving).

In the workplace, new companies are emerging to serve the needs of changing career spans and the changing nature of career arcs. Expect an explosion of reverse mentorships, when younger workers mentor older workers in a new stage after the older person retires from a career job. We will also see more returnships for people who have taken a career break.

Companies like J.P. Morgan, IBM, Facebook, Google, Amazon, and dozens more create these modified internships as a way to relaunch prior careers or to pivot to new roles. Intergenerational mentoring is more common as well. The secret sauce for many companies may become the wisdom harnessed across generations through such programs. For example, the movie *The Intern* spotlighted the value of reverse mentoring. Hotelier Chip Conley advocates for the modern elder in companies, modeling this role when he was head of global hospitality and strategy at Airbnb.[14]

The Longevity Project, developed in collaboration with the Stanford Center on Longevity, is also inviting companies, marketers, and thought leaders throughout the country to join a national conversation about the myriad needs and opportunities presented by longer lives. Significantly, the project has engaged both Gen Zers and millennials in the conversations on a range of needs. Topics in its podcasts include the future of work, reinventing cities, lifelong learning, financial security, lifelong health, longevity and the pandemic, ageism, longevity and equity, rethinking retirement, and caregiving.

There will also be intergenerational geographic opportunities. In February 2021, the *Boston Globe*, along with the founder of the MIT AgeLab, announced an effort to promote the Boston area as a new type of longevity hub for innovation. Citing the wealth of technology and health-care innovators, they believe that Boston could become the Silicon Valley of longevity. This type of intergenerational community could help accelerate the many innovations described in this book.[15]

In longevity circles, *intergenerational* is a hot term and hot concept, for good reason. The evidence is pouring in that focusing on these intergenerational interactions and collaborations pays for everyone. And we are just at the beginning of identifying the longevity dividends that will come from creating products and services that serve intergenerational needs.

• • •

It's a cliché in Silicon Valley to talk about the latest innovations as things that will make the world a better place, but in the longevity economy, this is not only truly possible but also necessary. The market opportunity is massive with longevity, no doubt. But without a focus on the impact potential, the market won't be fully realized.

The other side of the new longevity is the likelihood of a major economic and public health crisis if ageist attitudes persist and if policy isn't crafted thoughtfully. We can avoid such crises by investing in dignity and intergenerational opportunities.

As much as companies need imagination to create the new products and services to navigate a hundred-year life course, they must also be active participants in these policy innovations and actively embrace the opportunities. Doing so will enhance the impact of our new long-lived societies and enhance the longevity dividend.

● RECOMMENDATIONS

- Address ageism in your company's hiring practices, and recognize the value of older workers' contributions.

- Consider taking a longevity employer pledge for your company to actively combat ageist stereotypes in marketing and media.

- Redesign media and advertising when addressing the longevity market, or even intergenerational markets.

- Invest in dignity, and participate in the formulation of new policies and plans with government support for older adults that promote longevity.

- Become an age-ready organization by integrating policies to have a multigenerational workforce and providing data to support the increased value of multigenerational teams.

- Support the caregiving needs and paid family leave of your employees.

Furtherhood

If you have reached this conclusion you've learned quite a bit about the new longevity and the shift from thinking about the age of older adults to thinking about the stages they'll be living through as they enjoy longer lifespans and much longer healthspans. Think of it as your personal master class for understanding and entering the market.

And you may think that, with all the domains I've cited and all the companies we have examined, the problem is solved. It's not. It may seem as if the opportunities are all taken, but they aren't.

We are still in the early years of reimagining all the different ways hundred-year lives will affect the life course and how to best take advantage of an extra thirty or forty years of life. There is an overwhelming need for innovative solutions, new levels of access, and increasing affordability.

Modern aging is being recast as a vibrant opportunity and not just a problem to be solved. It is also a remarkable entrepreneurial opportunity, which will require understanding what people need and want to buy, the challenges they experience in getting to market, and some of the other roadblocks that can be addressed. I hope this book has provided you with those insights.

Innovation will need to occur around people's changing needs in the many stages of their longer lives. Will these needs have wider societal impacts for the new roadmaps of later life? It is hard to overstate the scope of the longevity market or the diversity of the longevity customers.

For example, the book didn't even consider autonomous vehicles for older adults who no longer want to or should drive, but such a market will grow significantly in the next ten-plus years. You can imagine that these vehicles may have certain amenities that promote their safety and accessibility and that appeal to an older adult or their family member. Communities that include many older adults will go to the places that support such innovations. Cities will plan around enabling this technology in their municipalities to attract people and the businesses that will serve them.

There will also be knowledge workers, such as lawyers, accountants, pathologists, and other professionals, who will want to stay engaged after turning sixty-five or older and want to work half time or at some other reduced level. Companies will need to help match their skills and interests to new opportunities, beyond the traditional full-time work. We'll need something like a Match.com for new ways to work and to help older adults with upskilling for continuous growth. If remote work becomes the norm for many companies, these opportunities will expand exponentially. As we increasingly see older adults as assets, all sorts of new opportunities will emerge to connect older people with younger as mentors, surrogate grandparents, and doers influencing society in many positive ways.

Imagine it is 2050, when there are more older adults than children under fifteen. We will absolutely need more and better ways to care for the older segment of the population but will have fewer resources to do so. Imagine there has been a complete overhaul of the caregiving system, that loneliness among older adults has been solved with new ways to connect older with younger people through a year of national service. Imagine that eighty-five-year-olds continue to be the fastest-growing population and that there are many new ways for them to engage in purposeful intergenerational communities. And there is longevity insurance, so that all can afford healthy aging and longevity. All these visions are truly possible if innovators both within companies and those starting new ones seize these opportunities.

One of the great challenges with longevity and categorizing stages for older adults has been finding the right words to use. From the challenges to coming up with nonageist, stage-focused appellations for older adults to defining terms like *olderpreneurs*—it is difficult to come up with words that are both adequately descriptive and not so awkward they call attention to themselves. Terms will continue to evolve.

I've adopted one such term: *furtherhood*. By no means do I think this is a great term, and I invite you to improve on it, but it's the one I use.

Furtherhood is not old age. It's not retirement age. It's not an age of impairments associated with aging bodies. Furtherhood is this new gift, this potential for thirty to forty years of life in which many more people will be healthy and active longer. It is the disruption to a century's old model of life—a model that no longer works.

I like this term, furtherhood, because it conveys imagining and redefining your own purpose through many further stages of life, evaluating how to contribute your wisdom, your values, and your experience to the next generations. It is not an ending but a series of new beginnings. My hope is that as you get older in life, you will not feel as though you are aging or ending but rather are going further to new opportunities and new possibilities. I hope you will consider embracing furtherhood as both a market and as part of your own lives.

When I started as a fellow in the Distinguished Careers Institute at Stanford, I thought I would devote the next chapter of my career to disrupting elder care. I felt awful after learning that my mother's end-of-life pain and suffering could have been prevented had she prepared a written advanced directive and had her wishes honored. I felt sad that she had been in the hospital so many times and yet a palliative care team did not see her until the day before she died. All of these steps could and should have been taken, but at the time I did not know how important they were nor how to navigate this for her.

I wanted to fix this situation for other families so that their loved ones would not go through the pain my mother did. I hoped they would not feel the same sorrow I had after someone they love does not have a good death.

But then I began to learn about the new longevity. About the importance of stage, not age. I discovered that there are so many new problems to be solved in addition to elder care and end-of-life planning, and so many innovation opportunities. Rather than focusing on one stage, end-of-life care, my mind was filled with excitement at all the possibilities. I saw my own journey through a new lens, as the many stages in my own life began to make sense in a new way. They came together in my own renaissance stage. My caregiving years, my public health career, my venture capital career, and my academic career all merged into a new purpose to help people live better longer lives and be well prepared and respected at the end of their life.

I could see it all so clearly. We will all go through many stages as we live far longer lives than our predecessors did. As we go further, I hope you will join me in this vibrant, dynamic, growing market and work to make a difference in a changing world. The opportunities are nearly endless.

APPENDIX

Stage Segmentation: The Eighteen Stages

Older adults are not a single market. When considering entering a longevity market, consider any number of stages the target consumer may be in. Keep in mind that they may be in more than one stage and that they may be a longevity customer even if they're not over sixty—as a caregiver, for example.

Table A-1, which I am reproducing from the table in chapter 2, presents my approach to the stages, but there are other stages. You may invent your own stages as well, basing them on your understanding of your customers.

TABLE A-1

The eighteen stages of life

Growth stages	Career and family stages	Reinvention stages	Closing stages
Starting	Continuous learning	Repurposing	Legacy
Growing	Developing financial security	Relaunching	End of life
First launch		Resetting life priorities	
	Parenting/family		
Experimenting			
	Caregiving	Transition	
	Optimizing health	Portfolio	
		Renaissance	
		Sidepreneur	

Demographic Segmentation:
The Five Quarters

The old three-phase model of life—learn, earn, retire—no longer holds as lifespans and healthspans increase. A new model maps the stages on top of a five-quarter, or 5Q, life. Under each quarter in figure A-1 (which is reproduced from chapter 2), people will find themselves in multiple stages concurrently. For example, caregiving could take place in Q2 and Q4. Learning will most certainly span nearly every stage. When building a longevity strategy, businesses should map target customers to their stages and demographic quarter.

FIGURE A-1

The five-quarter (5Q) life framework

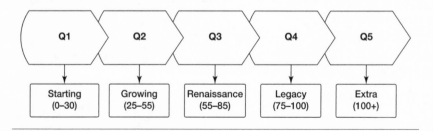

Domain Segmentation: Markets to Target

Virtually every market domain will be affected by the new longevity, that is, increased lifespans and healthspans, but some domains have emerged faster than others. Table A-2 summarizes key domains for products and services we have discussed, as well as some additional ones that stem from the different life-stage priorities outlined in chapter 3. Use these domains to further refine your longevity strategy.

TABLE A-2

Markets to target

Life-stage priorities	Emerging product and service domains	Examples of subdomains
Home and housing	Home modifications	Preparing homes to be longevity ready
	Housing alternatives	Intergenerational housing and cohousing
Money and security	Financial services	Financial products for lifelong learning; women and financial planning; financial caregiving
	Fintech	Prevention of fraud and elder abuse
	Insuretech	Insurance navigation; Medicare Advantage navigation
Health and longevity	Longevity health services	Longevity health assessments and checkups
	Food and nutrition	Food preparation/delivery
	Fitness and wellness	Remote fitness programs
	Telehealth	Specialist care and technology; hospital in the home; remote patient monitoring
Caregiving and family	Care navigation	Care coordination and transition planning; caregiver quality of life; financial caregiving
	Long-term care	In-home care services and technology
	Memory care	Devices
Purpose and giving	Social health/ community service	Long-life learning programs; isolation and loneliness support; intergenerational activities; new types of work; matching services for skills and interests
Spirituality and identity	End-of-life planning	Palliative care; advance care planning; funeral planning; legacy
Learning and connection	Continuous learning	Digital literacy; digital health; digital access; life-transition planning; midcareer learning programs
Civic life and community	Intergenerational connection/volunteering	Matching services/platforms for engagement; volunteering platforms

Within each of these domains are often multiple subdomains. For example, under the financial services domain, there are subdomains that address financial planning and the prevention of fraud and financial abuse among older adults.

For caregiving, I have identified no fewer than twenty-six subdomains, including these: care navigation and transitions; care coordination; caregiver quality of life; daily essential activities for the care recipient; health and safety awareness; social well-being; isolation and loneliness prevention; wellness; smart home; wearables; fall prevention, fall detection; mobility; fitness; sensory aids; transportation; medication management; tech-enabled home care; financial caregiving; end-of-life care and planning; insurance and reimbursement; cognitive care; housing; diet and nutrition; digital inclusion, access, and literacy; and telehealth for older adults.

Defining Your Longevity Opportunity

Successful entry into the longevity market requires a deliberate approach that actively avoids the idea of making products and services for older people. The following important steps to develop a deliberate approach are taken from the best practices of the companies discussed in this book.

- Need: Define what problem or challenge needs to be addressed. Do not assume the need is based on declining health or ability. For example, there is a massive need for education solutions for older adults.

- Opportunity: Define the market opportunities by analyzing gaps in the market, the size of the market, and its relationship to your capabilities or the capabilities you want to develop. For example, if you make or design home fitness equipment, learn about how many older adults participate and what their economic and demographic profile is.

- User: Think carefully about who the user is, remembering that they may not be the customer or the payer. They may not even be over sixty. For example, the user may be a midcareer person in their thirties planning finances for later in life.

- Stages: Define the stages of the customer you want to target. Learn about the characteristics and dynamics of people in these specific stages. For example, what do olderpreneurs value, and what is missing from entrepreneurial products they need?

- Domains: Define the domains and subdomains. Try to home in on specific opportunities. For example, don't focus on telehealth as a market opportunity; focus on telehealth in rural areas for older adults aging in place.

- Payer: Define who pays for the product or service, remembering that it's not always the end user or the customer you market to. For example, companies that want to offer caregiving leave benefits need to understand how to interact with insurance providers as payers.

- Acquisition challenges: Identify the obstacles to gaining customers. For example, if you're a builder trying to build housing for aging in place, are local building codes difficult to manage?

- Ageism: Be sure to combat your own and others' biases and stereotypes about the target customer. Don't focus on demographics as an identifying characteristic unless you have to. Don't use ageist language. Beware of making faulty assumptions about the users. For example, some people mistakenly assume that older adults are not only less adept with technology but also less willing to learn technology. This isn't true.

- **Channel challenges:** Identify which gaps in the channel will make it difficult to execute your plan. Work to build and support platforms that will connect customers to products and services more easily than they do now. For example, in one exercise around caregiving, my colleagues and I identified fifteen companies that were using nine different channels in multiple combinations to reach customers. This complicated web is inefficient and expensive.

- **Funding:** Marshal the resources to fund your product or service. At large companies, funding could come from an internal champion or a budget from an innovation fund. At startups, focus on the venture capital community and its increasing focus on this opportunity.

- **Scale:** If you succeed with a single product or service, look for opportunities to grow that success into other areas serving other customers in different stages. For example, a fashion company that successfully sold yoga pants for older adults in a renaissance stage may take what it learned, along with new learning, to offer footwear or even exercise classes.

The Entrepreneur's Opportunities

The venture capital and entrepreneurial communities are increasingly turning to the longevity market as a vast opportunity. Table A-3 shows some of that activity and can serve as inspiration for entrepreneurs who are looking to pitch their ideas to venture capitalists.

Entrepreneurial interest will only grow as more exits (investments that succeed by being acquired or going public) achieve results like those shown in table A-4.

TABLE A-3

Examples of venture firms investing in the longevity market

Investor	Selected investments
7wireVentures	Homethrive
Andreesen Horowitz (a16z)	Honor; Tomorrow Health; Bold; Devoted Health
Battery Ventures	A Place for Mom; ClearCare
Blue Venture Fund	Wider Circle
Canaan	Papa
Comcast Ventures	Papa
Emerson Collective	Tembo Health; GoodTrust; FreeWill
Generator Ventures	ActiveProtective; CareLinx; Caremerge; True Link Financial; Vesta Healthcare; Vynca; Wellthy
GoAhead Ventures	Cake
GSR Ventures	Cherry Labs
Kaiser Permanente Ventures	Vesta Healthcare; SilverLink
Lightspeed Venture Partners	Curve Health
Magnify Ventures	Papa
Maverick Ventures	Mon Ami; Devoted Health; Castlight; Chapter
NEA	SafeRide Health
Oak HC/FT	Vesta Healthcare; Modern Age; CareBridge; Devoted Health
OCA Ventures	Cake; Vynca
Pillar VC	Cake
Portfolia	Cake
Primetime Partners	Bold; Carewell; Tembo Health; Bloom; GetSetUp; Retirable
Rethink Impact	Wellthy; CareAcademy
Rise of the Rest Seed Fund	Cariloop
SoftBank Vision Fund	Papa; Devoted Health
Springbank Collective	Wellthy; AloeCare
Thrive Capital	Umbrella; Honor
Tiger Global Management	Papa
Town Hall Ventures	WelbeHealth; Signify Health
Two Lanterns Venture Partners	Cake
Ziegler Link-Age Longevity Fund	BlueStar SeniorTech; Breezie; CareLinx; Caremerge; Cosán; Embodied Labs; Forefront Telecare; Health-PRO Heritage; Included Health; Ingenios Health; K4Connect; LifeSite; Minka; OnShift; Payactiv; Prodigo Solutions; PS Lifestyle; Socially Determined; Strategic Health Care; Third Eye Health; True Link; VirtuSense; VitalTech; Vynca

TABLE A-4

**Investment exits from entrepreneurial opportunities
in the longevity market**

Company	IPO, acquirer, or lead investor	Year	Valuation	Transaction
InnovAge	Apax Partners	2020	$950 million	Acquisition
True Link	Khosla Ventures	2020	$135 million	Series B
Silvernest	Incenter (Finance of America)	2020	Undisclosed	Acquisition
Care.com*	—	2014	$550 million ($17 per share)	IPO
PillPack	Amazon	2018	$750 million	Acquisition
GreatCall	Best Buy	2018	$800 million	Acquisition
Current Health	Best Buy	2021	$400 million	Acquistion
CareLinx	Generali Global Assistance	2017	Undisclosed	Acquisition
Ingenios Health	Almost Family	2015	$13.4 million	Acquisition
Living Independently Group	GE Healthcare	2009	Undisclosed	Acquisition
SilverSneakers	Tivity Health	2006	$450 million	Acquisition

Note: data is current as of November 2021.

*Care.com was acquired by IAC in 2019 for $500 million ($15 per share).

Innovation Gaps and Opportunities

It can't be stated enough that there are virtually infinite possibilities in the longevity market, and there will be opportunities and needs we haven't even conceived of yet as the population makes its massive demographic shift.

Still, early in this shift, some marketing strategies have emerged faster because of market gaps that have been exposed when people needing products and services either don't have them or can't find them.

The following sections are inexhaustive illustrations of some of the most pressing gaps to inspire your thinking on developing your own longevity market opportunity.

Housing and Home Modification Services and Products

Example: Stairs

More than 90 percent of older adults want to age in place. How can we reconfigure access in homes? What are simpler and less costly solutions—the new "drone" of stairway access? What are the most essential modifications that all construction and renovation should consider? How can construction and renovation companies supply creative solutions? Preparing homes to be longevity ready is one business opportunity.

Housing Alternatives

Example: Intergenerational Housing

Creative cohabitation tackles many longevity challenges at once, from aging in place to loneliness prevention, caregiving, and intergenerational learning. The model can work with an increased emphasis on platforms that support customer acquisition and ongoing management.

Longevity Health Services in the Home

Example: Telehealth and Caregiving

Telehealth came of age in the pandemic but is not going anywhere afterward. The world's changing demographics will need more companies that feature easy access, quality control, continuity of care, and clear reimbursement mechanisms. Tailoring products and services to the "hospital in the home" addresses both an innovation gap and a market opportunity.

Digital Health and Wellness Tools and Assessment

Example: Sensors and Monitoring Technology

Aging in place will require the kinds of easy assessment of older adults that allows interventions when necessary. Sensors connected to algorithms that, say, know how often a refrigerator is being opened are the kinds of monitors that will enable successful aging in place.

Fintech

Example: Financial Abuse Prevention

The opportunity here is plain: losses from financial abuse are more than $9 billion per year in the United States. Financial abuse is considered the crime of the twenty-first century. During the Covid-19 pandemic there was a major increase in financial elder abuse. More companies and services are needed to prevent and detect this kind of crime, which is sometimes committed by trusted family members.

Care Navigation and Coordination

Example: Medicare Advantage Navigation

In many longevity markets, there are plenty of resources, products, and services available, but they are weakly coordinated, hard to find, and difficult to manage. For example, the number of decisions and purchases made around end-of-life care and planning is dizzying. Companies that can coordinate the navigation of disparate needs within any domain will find huge opportunities. Another possibility for innovation is Medicare and Medicare Advantage programs, which are complex, hard to navigate, and, therefore, often underutilized.

Social Health

Example: Caregiver Burnout

This is a challenge for both older adults and caregivers. Caregiver burnout is among the subdomains in need of innovation. Telling a caregiver to do more self-care and to exercise presents a conundrum: the caregiver is hampered by a lack of time and insufficient numbers of respite services. Opportunities are there for companies that can weave wellness for caregivers into the caregiving ecosystem. Isolation and loneliness among older adults remains an important area in need of innovative solutions.

End-of-Life Planning

Example: Planning Tools

End-of-life planning involves many subdomains, including legal document management, advance care planning, palliative and hospice care, funeral and burial planning, and legacy. This sector could greatly benefit from platforms, and they are emerging. However, end-of-life planning continues to be an underserved area with a large market opportunity. More intergenerational tools and guides (e.g., the Conversation Project) will be enhanced if they could be made more family-friendly. Only 37 percent of Americans have advance directives for end-of-life care. Much more can be done to create dignity at this stage.

Platforms

This need underscores all longevity opportunities. For all the development of the market so far, it's wildly various and uncoordinated. Companies continue to struggle to match their products and services with older adults and caregivers efficiently. Creating an integrated system where companies could list and promote their services and products, and where older adults and caregivers could have access to these offerings, would greatly reduce the gaps in our caregiving system. AI-enhanced tools could match people and solutions according to their needs for care and their profiles.

Resources for Entrepreneurs

Innovation Hubs and Labs

Entrepreneurs looking to evaluate their product and service ideas have an increasing number of communities and idea labs to turn to, including the following:

AgeTech Collaborative, sponsored by AARP and its Innovation Labs (https://agetechcollaborative.org/)

Avenidas (https://www.avenidas.org/)

Longevity Explorers (https://www.techenhancedlife.com/)

Milken Institute Center for the Future of Aging (https://milkeninstitute.org/centers/center-for-the-future-of-aging)

MIT AgeLab: Lifestyle Leaders (https://agelab.mit.edu/get-involved/panels/85-lifestyle-leaders-panel/)

SilverLife (https://www.silverlife.co)

Techstars Future of Longevity Accelerator (https://www.techstars.com/accelerators/longevity)

The Villages Movement (https://www.vtvnetwork.org/)

Newsletters and Websites

Age in Place Tech (https://www.ageinplacetech.com/)

Age Tech and the Gerontechnologist
(https://www.thegerontechnologist.com/)

ATI Advisory: Anne Tumlinson Innovations
(https://atiadvisory.com)

Better Health While Aging, by Leslie Kernisan, MD
(https://betterhealthwhileaging.net/leslie-kernisan-md-mph/)

Daughterhood (https://www.daughterhood.org/)

Family Caregiving Alliance (https://www.caregiver.org/)

Leading Age (https://leadingage.org/)

MFA Longevity Market Report (https://www.maryfurlong.com)

National Institute on Aging (https://www.nia.nih.gov/)

Next Avenue (https://www.nextavenue.org/)

OATS (Older Adult Technology Services) (https://oats.org/)

Senior Planet (https://seniorplanet.org/)

Stanford Center on Longevity Design Challenge
(https://longevity.stanford.edu/design-challenge)

The Center on Aging & Work at Boston College (https://www
.bc.edu/content/bc-web/schools/ssw/sites/center-on-aging-and
-work.html)

The Conversation Project (https://theconversationproject.org/)

The Hartford Foundation (https://www.johnahartford.org/)

The Scan Foundation and Alive Ventures
(https://www.thescanfoundation.org/)

Resources and Initiatives to Address Ageism

AARP, "Employer Pledge Program: Demonstrate Your Commitment to Experienced Workers" (www.aarp.org/work/job-search/employer-pledge-companies)

End Ageism, San Francisco Awareness Campaign (https://endageism.com/why-does-ageism-matter)

Frameworks Institute, "Aging, Agency, and Attribution of Responsibility," Moira O'Neil and Abigail Haydon (www.frameworksinstitute.org)

Mercer, "Are You Age-Ready?" (https://www.mercer.com/our-thinking/next-stage-are-you-age-ready.html)

Reframing Aging.org (https://www.reframingaging.org/) and Quick Start Guide (https://www.reframingaging.org/Portals/gsa-ra/QuickStartGuide_PrintReady_REV.pdf)

Sages and Seekers Inc., "Developing Empathy, Diminishing Ageism" (https://Sagesandseekers.site)

Wisdom at Work: Top Ten Practices for Becoming an Age Friendly Employer, Chip Conley, 2018

World Health Organization, "Global Campaign to Combat Ageism" (https://www.who.int/teams/social-determinants-of-health/demographic-change-and-healthy-ageing/combatting-ageism/global-report-on-ageism)

World Health Organization, "Global Report on Ageism— Executive Summary 2021" (https://www.who.int/publications/i/item/9789240020504)

United Nations, "Global Campaign to Combat Ageism Toolkit" (https://www.decadeofhealthyageing.org/find-knowledge/support/toolkits)

Resources on Caregiving

AARP, "Prepare to Care: A Planning Guide for Families" (https://assets.aarp.org/www.aarp.org_/articles/foundation /aa66r2_care.pdf)

AARP and National Alliance for Caregiving, "Caregiving in the United States 2020" (doi.10.26419-2Fppi.00103.001.pdf)

AARP and Project Catalyst Parks Associates, "Caregiving Innovation Frontiers" (https://www.aarp.org/research/topics/care /info-2019/caregiving-innovation-frontiers.html)

AARP, Family Caregiving (www.aarp.org/caregiving)

Family Caregiving Alliance (https://www.caregiver.org)

Holding Co. and Pivotal Ventures, "Investor's Guide to the Care Economy, July 2021" (Investin.care)

Susan Golden and the dciX Caregiving Innovations Group, "Landscape of Caregiving Innovations" (https://dci.stanford.edu /wp-content/uploads/2021/11/Landscape-of-Caregiving -Innovations-Report-1.pdf.)

Reading List

Books

Carstensen, Laura L. *A Long Bright Future: Happiness, Health, and Financial Security in an Age of Increased Longevity.* New York: Public Affairs, 2011.

Chatzky, Jean, and Michael E. Roizen. *Ageproof: Living Longer without Running Out of Money or Breaking a Hip.* New York: Grand Central Publishing, 2017.

Conley, Chip, *Wisdom@Work: The Making of a Modern Elder*. New York: Currency, 2018.

Coughlin, Joseph F. *The Longevity Economy: Unlocking the World's Fastest-Growing, Most Misunderstood Market*. New York: Public Affairs, 2017.

Farrell, Chris. *Unretirement: How Baby Boomers Are Changing the Way We Think About Work, Community, and the Good Life*. New York: Bloomsbury, 2014.

Freedman, Marc. *How to Live Forever: The Enduring Power of Connecting the Generations*. New York: Public Affairs, 2018.

Gawande, Atul. *Being Mortal: Medicine and What Matters in the End*. New York: Metropolitan Books, 2014.

Gratton, Lynda, and Andrew Scott. *The 100-Year Life: Living and Working in an Age of Longevity*. New York: Bloomsbury, 2016.

Irving, Paul H. *The Upside of Aging: How Long Life Is Changing the World of Health, Work, Innovation, Policy, and Purpose*. Hoboken, NJ: Wiley, 2014.

Jenkins, Jo Ann. *Disrupt Aging: A Bold New Path to Living Your Best Life at Every Age*. New York: Public Affairs, 2016.

Miller, Bruce J., and Shoshana Berger. *A Beginner's Guide to the End: Practical Advice for Living Life and Facing Death*. New York: Simon & Shuster, 2019.

Pantilat, Steven Z. *Life after the Diagnosis: Expert Advice on Living Well with Serious Illness for Patients and Caregivers*. Boston: Da Capo Lifelong Books, 2017.

Poo, Ai-Jen. *The Age of Dignity: Preparing for the Elder Boom in a Changing America*. New York: The New Press, 2015.

Sinclair, David A. *Lifespan: Why We Age—and Why We Don't Have To*. New York: Harper Collins, 2019.

Reports

Accius, Jean, and Joo Yeoun Suh. "The Economic Impact of Age Discrimination: How Discriminating Against Older Workers Could Cost the U.S. Economy $850 Billion." Washington, DC: AARP Thought Leadership, January 2020. https://doi.org/10.26419/int.00042.003.

Accius, Jean, and Joo Yeoun Suh. "The Economic Impact of Supporting Working Family Caregivers." Washington, DC: AARP Thought Leadership, March 2021. https://doi.org/10.26419/int.00042.006.

Accius, Jean and Joo Yeoun Suh. "The Longevity Economy Outlook: How People Age 50 and Older Are Fueling Economic Growth, Stimulating Jobs, and Creating Opportunities for All." Washington DC: AARP Thought Leadership, December 2019. https://doi.org/10.26419/int.00042.001.

Global Campaign to Combat Ageism. "Global Report on Ageism." Geneva: World Health Organization, 2021. www.who.int/teams/social-determinants-of-health/demographic-change-and-healthy-ageing/combatting-ageism/global-report-on-ageism.

Irving, Paul. "Silver to Gold: The Business of Aging." Milken Institute Center for the Future of Aging. 2018. https://milkeninstitute.org/report/silve-gold-business-aging.

Orlov, Laurie M. "The Future of Remote Care Technology and Older Adults: Connection Is Everything." *Aging in Place Technology Watch*, November 2020. www.ageinplacetech.com/page/future-remote-care-technology-and-older-adults-2020.

Stanford Center on Longevity. "The New Map of Life: 100 Years to Thrive." Report from Stanford Center on Longevity, November 2021. https://longevity.stanford.edu/wp-content/uploads/2021/11/NMOL_report_FINAL-5.pdf.

Woodard, Monique. "Gray New World. 2020 Report on Aging." CakeMX. www.graynewworld.com.

Articles

Agarwal, Medha. "The $740 Billion Senior Care Market Is Ripe for Disruption, but Full of Challenges." Redpoint, November 30, 2016. https://medium.com/redpoint-ventures/the-740-billion-senior-care-market-is-ripe-for-disruption-but-full-of-challenges-a13e3b53548.

AgeLab. "Caregiving & Wellbeing." Massachusetts Institute of Technology, 2019. https://agelab.mit.edu/caregiving-wellbeing.

Berg, Peter, and Matthew Piszczek. "Retirement-Proof Your Company." *Harvard Business Review*, November 14, 2018. https://hbr.org/2018/11/retirement-proof-your-company.

Bianchi, Nicola, Jin Li, and Michael Powell. "What Happens to Younger Workers When Older Workers Don't Retire." *Harvard Business Review*, November 16, 2018. https://hbr.org/2018/11/what-happens-to-younger-workers-when-older-workers-dont-retire.

Engelhart, Katie. "What Robots Can—and Can't—Do for the Old and Lonely." *New Yorker*, May 24, 2021. www.newyorker.com/magazine/2021/05/31/what-robots-can-and-cant-do-for-the-old-and-lonely.

Gates, Melinda. "How Rethinking Caregiving Could Play a Crucial Role in Restarting the Economy." *Washington Post*, May 7, 2020. https://www.washingtonpost.com/opinions/2020/05/07/melinda-gates-how-rethinking-caregiving-could-play-crucial-role-restarting-economy/.

Gupta, Sarita, and Ai-jen Poo. "Caring for Your Company's Caregivers." *Harvard Business Review*, November 13, 2018. https://hbr.org/2018/11/caring-for-your-companys-caregivers.

Irving, Paul. "The Longevity Opportunity." *Harvard Business Review*, November 8, 2018. https://hbr.org/2018/11/the-longevity-opportunity.

Irving, Paul. "When No One Retires." *Harvard Business Review*, November 7, 2018. https://hbr.org/2018/11/when-no-one-retires.

Khabbaz, Ramsey, and Matt Perry. "Just How Old Are We Getting?" *Harvard Business Review*, November 15, 2018. https://hbr.org/2018/11/just-how-old-are-we-getting.

Miller, Stephen. "Caregiving Benefits Tend to Miss the Mark." *SHRM*, January 22, 2019. www.shrm.org/resourcesandtools/hr-topics /benefits/pages/caregiving-benefits-miss-the-mark.aspx.

Tapen, Colleen. "Rethinking Retraining." *Harvard Business Review*, November 9, 2018. https://hbr.org/2018/11/rethinking-retraining.

Tognola, Glenn. "How to Prepare Your Financial Information for When You Die." *Wall Street Journal*, October 3, 2020. www.wsj.com /articles/how-to-prepare-your-financial-information-for-when-you -die-11601697960.

Washington, Kate. "50 Million Americans Are Unpaid Caregivers. We Need Help." *New York Times*, February 2021. https://www.nytimes .com/2021/02/22/opinion/us-caregivers-biden.html.

NOTES

Chapter 1

1. Gerontological Society of America, "Longevity Economics: Leveraging the Advantages of an Aging Society," August 6, 2018, https://www.geron.org/images/gsa/documents/gsa-longevity-economics-2018.pdf.

2. AARP and Oxford Economics, "The Longevity Economy: How People Over 50 Are Driving Economic and Social Value in the US," September 2016, https://www.oxfordeconomics.com/recent-releases/the-longevity-economy; and Gerontological Society of America, "Longevity Economics."

3. US Census Bureau, "An Aging Nation: Projected Number of Children and Older Adults in the United States," Census Infographics and Visualizations, March 13, 2018, www.census.gov/library/visualizations/2018/comm/historic-first.html; and US Census Bureau, "From Pyramid to Pillar: A Century of Change, Population of the U.S.," Census Infographic and Visualizations, March 13, 2018, www.census.gov/library/visualizations/2018/comm/century-of-change.html.

4. US Census Bureau, "From Pyramid to Pillar."

5. Thomas Rando, "Aging, Rejuvenation, and Epigenetic Reprogramming: Resetting the Aging Clock," *Cell* 148, no. 1 (2012): 46–57, 2012.

6. Wolfgang Fengler, "Living into the 22nd Century," Brookings, January 14, 2020, https://www.brookings.edu/blog/future-development/2020/01/14/living-into-the-22nd-century/.

7. Lauren Medina, S. Sabo, and J. Vespa, "Living Longer: Historical and Projected Life Expectancy in the United States, 1960 to 2060," United States Census Bureau, February 2020; and Eileen M. Crimmins, "Lifespan and Healthspan: Past, Present and Promise," *Gerontologist* 55, no. 6 (2015).

8. K. Kochanek, X. Jiaquan, and E. Arias, "Mortality in the United States, 2019," *NCHS Data Brief* 395 (December 2020): 1–8.

9. "The Future of Aging? The New Drugs &Tech Working to Extend Life & Wellness," research report, CB Insights, October 24, 2018.

10. Health Resources & Services Administration, "The 'Loneliness Epidemic,'" January 2019, https://www.hrsa.gov/enews/past-issues/2019/january-17/loneliness-epidemic.

11. L. L. Carstensen, *A Long Bright Future: Happiness, Health and Financial Security in an Age of Longevity* (New York: Broadway Books, 2009), 16–20.

12. National Council on Aging, "Get the Facts on Economic Security for Seniors," March 1, 2021, https://www.ncoa.org/article/get-the-facts-on-economic-security -for-seniors.

13. Mercer Global, "Are You Age-Ready?," white paper, 2019, www .mercer.com/our-thinking/next-stage-are-you-age-ready.html.

14. Stanford Center on Longevity, "The New Map of Life: 100 Years to Thrive," https://longevity.stanford.edu/the-new-map-of-life-initiative.

Chapter 2

1. Harriet Edleson, "More Americans Working Past 65," AARP, April 22, 2019, www.aarp.org/work/employers/info-2019/americans-working-past-65.html.

2. J. Accius, and Joo Yeoun Suh, "The Longevity Economy Outlook: How People Age 50 and Older Are Fueling Economic Growth, Stimulating Jobs, and Creating Opportunities for All," AARP Thought Leadership and Oxford Economics, December 2019.

3. Joe Pinsker, "When Does Someone Become 'Old'?," *Atlantic*, January 27, 2020, https://www.theatlantic.com/family/archive/2020/01/old-people-older-elderly -middle-age/605590/.

4. Arthur Brettschneider, "Tech Entrepreneurs: How to Market to the Growing Senior Population," *Forbes*, March 11, 2019, https://www.forbes.com/sites /theyec/2019/03/11/tech-entrepreneurs-how-to-market-to-the-growing-senior -population/?sh=4d7fda9741e0.

5. Derek Ozkal, "Millennials Can't Keep Up with Boomer Entrepreneurs," *Currents* (Ewing Marion Kauffman Foundation), July 19, 2016, www.kauffman.org /currents/age-and-entrepreneurship.

6. US Census Bureau, "2018 Annual Business Survey (ABS) Program," released May 19, 2020, https://www.census.gov/content/dam/Census/library/visualizations /2020/comm/business-owners-ages.pdf.

7. American Express, "2019 State of Women-Owned Businesses Report," September 2019, https://s1.q4cdn.com/692158879/files/doc_library/file/2019-state-of -women-owned-businesses-report.pdf, page 8.

8. Gerontological Society of America, "Longevity Economics: Leveraging the Advantages of an Aging Society," report, August 6, 2018, 2, www.geron.org/images /gsa/documents/gsa-longevity-economics-2018.pdf; and Joe Kita, "Age Discrimination Still Thrives in America," AARP, December 30, 2019, www.aarp.org/work /working-at-50-plus/info-2019/age-discrimination-in-america.html.

9. Reframing Aging San Francisco campaign, October 16, 2019, https://endageism .com; and World Health Organization, "Global Campaign to Combat Ageism," https://www.un.org/development/desa/dspd/wp-content/uploads/sites/22/2021/03 /global-campaign-to-combat-ageism-toolkit-en.pdf and "Global Report on Ageism:

Executive Summary," March 2021, https://www.who.int/publications/i/item
/9789240020504.

10. Catherine Collinson, "Wishful Thinking or Within Reach? Three Generations
Prepare for 'Retirement,'" 18th Annual Transamerica Retirement Survey of Workers,
Transamerica Center for Retirement Studies, report 1355-1217, December 2017.

Chapter 3

1. For example, platforms that segment the longevity and aging market include:
the Gerontechnologist, Age Tech Market Map (www.thegerontechnologist.com);
the AgeTech Collaborative, sponsored by the AARP and its Innovation Labs
(https://agtechcollaborative.org); and the Aging2.0 Collective (www.aging2.com).
See the appendix for more details.

2. Administration for Community Living, 2020 Profile of Older Americans, May
2021, https://acl.gov/aging-and-disability-in-america/data-and-research/profile-older
-americans; and AARP and Oxford Economics, "The Longevity Economy: How
People Over 50 Are Driving Economic and Social Value in the US," September 2016,
https://www.oxfordeconomics.com/recent-releases/the-longevity-economy.

3. Gerontological Society of America, "Longevity Economics: Leveraging the
Advantages of an Aging Society," August 6, 2018, www.geron.org/images/gsa
/documents/gsa-longevity-economics-2018.pdf.

4. Gerontological Society of America, "Retirement Structures and Processes,"
Public Policy and Aging Report 31, no. 3 (2021).

5. Nadia Tuma-Weldon, "Truth About Age," McCann Truth Central, 2018.

6. Tuma-Weldon, "Truth About Age."

7. Susan Conley, "Longevity Market Map," Stria News, 2019.

8. Aging2.0 brings together corporations, startups, researchers, governments,
and older people themselves to explore how technology can help transform the aging
experience. Key focus areas so far have been the digital divide, family caregiving,
and shifting care to the community. It is now run by the Louisville Healthcare CEO
Council as their Global Innovation arm. Aging2.0, "Annual Report 2018–2019," www
.aging2.com/grandchallenges.

9. Jean Accius and Joo Yeoun Suh, "The Longevity Economy Outlook: How
People Ages 50 and Older Are Fueling Economic Growth, Stimulating Jobs, and Creating Opportunities for All," Washington, DC: AARP Thought Leadership, December
2019, https://doi.org/10.26419/int.00042.001; Kauffman Indicators of Entrepreneurship, 2018 National Report on Early-Stage Entrepreneurship, September 2019,
https://www.realclearpublicaffairs.com/ib; and Pierre Azoulay, Benjamin F. Jones, J.
Daniel Kim, and Javier Miranda, "The Average Age of a Startup Founder Is 45," *Harvard
Business Review*, July 11, 2018, https://hbr.org/2018/07/research-the-average-age-of-a
-successful-startup-founder-is-45.

10. Danny McDermott, quoted in Carol Hymowitz, "The First MBA Course on the Longevity Economy," *Next Avenue*, March 24, 2020, www.nextavenue.org /first-mba-class-longevity-economy.

Chapter 4

1. Susan Golden and Laura. L. Carstensen, "How Merrill Lynch Is Planning for Its Customers to Live to 100," *Harvard Business Review*, March 4, 2019.

2. Golden and Carstensen, "How Merrill Lynch Is Planning for Its Customers to Live to 100."

3. Lavanya Nair, "This Increasing Client Risk Will Change Advisor Practices. Here's Why," FinancialPlanning, March 12, 2019, https://www.financial-planning .com/news/schwab-study-cites-longevity-as-most-impactful-on-advisor-firms.

4. For example, Silvur, Golden Seeds, and Golden (joingolden.com).

5. Andy Sieg, "Longevity: The Economic Opportunity of Our Lifetime," *Forbes*, December 16, 2016, https://www.forbes.com/sites/nextavenue/2016/12/16/longevity -the-economic-opportunity-of-our-lifetime; and Surya Koluri, interview with author, July 2018.

6. Merrill Lynch Bank of America Corporation and Age Wave, "Women & Financial Wellness: Beyond the Bottom Line," 2018, www.ml.com/registration/women -and-financial-wellness.html.

7. Jeffrey Hall, Debra Karch, and Alex Crosby, *Uniform Definitions and Recommended Core Data Elements for Use in Elder Abuse Surveillance* (Atlanta: National Center for Injury Prevention and Control, 2016).

8. Lori A. Stiegel and Mary Joy Quinn, "Elder Abuse: The Impact of Undue Influence," issue brief, American Bar Association and National Center on Law and Elder Rights, June 2017.

9. Robert Chess and Jeffrey Conn, "Nike: Sport Forever," Case E690 (Stanford, CA: Stanford Graduate School of Business, 2020).

10. Neil Blumenthal, interview with author, September 2020.

11. Neil Blumenthal, interview with author, September 2020.

12. Project Catalyst, Parks Associates, AARP Research, "Can 40 Million Caregivers Count on You? Caregiving Innovation Frontiers," AARP, June 2017.

13. For the cigarette comparison, see J. Holt-Lunstad, T. B. Smith, and J. B. Layton, "Social Relationships and Mortality Risk: A Meta-Analytic Review," *PLOS Medicine*, July 27, 2010.

14. Vivek Murthy, "Work and the Loneliness Epidemic," *Harvard Business Review*, September 26, 2017, https://hbr.org/2017/09/work-and-the-loneliness-epidemic.

15. Wider Circle, "Wider Circle Raises $38m in Series B Funding Led by Ameri-Health Caritas," press release, September 29, 2021, www.widercircle.com /blog/wider-circle-raises-38m-in-series-b-funding-round-led-by-amerihealth-caritas/.

16. Darin Buxbaum, interview with author, October 27, 2020.

17. Philip A. Pizzo, "A Prescription for Longevity in the 21st Century: Renewing Purpose, Building and Sustaining Social Engagement, and Embracing a Positive Lifestyle," *JAMA*, January 9, 2020.

18. Ari Levy, "Teledoc and Livongo Merge into $37 Billion Remote-Health Company as Coronavirus Keeps Patients Home," *CNBC*, August 5, 2020.

19. Lauri Orlov, "Remote Care Technology and Older Adults: Filling In the Basics 2020," *Aging and Health Technology Watch* (blog), www.Ageinplacetech.com, November 11, 2020.

20. AARP and National Alliance for Caregiving, "Caregiving in the United States," May 14, 2020, https://www.aarp.org/ppi/info-2020/caregiving-in-the-united-states.html.

21. The Holding Co. and Pivotal Ventures, "Investor's Guide to the Care Economy," 2021, https://www.investin.care/.

22. Techstars, "Techstars Future of Longevity Accelerator," https://www.techstars.com/accelerators/longevity; Techstars, "Techstars and Pivotal Ventures to Launch Longevity Accelerator," press release, January 6, 2020, www.techstars.com/newsroom/techstars-and-pivotal-ventures-to-launch-longevity-accelerator.

23. Cision, "Techstars Announces Future of Longevity Class of 2021," press release, November 10, 2021, https://www.prweb.com/releases/techstars_announces_future_of_longevity_class_of_2021/prweb18323603.htm.

24. Susan Golden et al., "Landscape of Caregiving Innovations," Stanford Distinguished Careers Institute (DCI) and dciX, September 2021, https://dci.stanford.edu/wp-content/uploads/2021/11/Landscape-of-Caregiving-Innovations-Report-1.pdf.

25. Randy Klein, interview with author, December 2020.

26. Lindsay Jurist-Rosner, interview with author, February 2021.

27. M. J. Field, C. K. Cassel, eds., *Approaching Death: Improving Care at the End of Life* (Washington, DC: National Academies Press, 1997).

28. Robert Chess, Susan Golden, and Jack Strabo, "Cake: Navigating Mortality," Case E744 (Stanford, CA: Stanford Graduate School of Business, 2021); see also www.joincake.com.

29. Suelin Chen, interview with author, July 2020; and Chess, Golden, and Strabo, "Cake."

30. Mark Silverman, interview with author, December 7, 2020.

31. Robert Urstein, interview with author, January 2021.

Chapter 5

1. Sidney Katz, "Assessing Self-Maintenance: Activities of Daily Living, Mobility, and Instrumental Activities of Daily Living," *J AM Geriatric Society* 31, no. 12 (1983):721–727; and Peter F. Edemekong, Deb L. Bomgaars, Sukesh Sukumaran, and Shoshana B. Levy, "Activities of Daily Living," StatPearls, September 26, 2021, https://www.ncbi.nlm.nih.gov/books/NBK470404/.

2. Liz O'Donnell, *Working Daughter: A Guide to Caring for Your Aging Parents While Making a Living* (Lanham, MD: Rowman & Littlefield, 2019).

3. Joseph B. Fuller and Manjari Raman, "The Caring Company: How Employers Can Help Employees Manage Their Caregiving Responsibilities—While Reducing Costs and Increasing Productivity," Harvard Business School Project on Managing the Future of Work, updated January 17, 2019.

4. Tiffany Hsu, "Older People Are Ignored and Distorted in Ageist Marketing, Report Finds," *New York Times*, September 23, 2019, https://www.nytimes.com /2019/09/23/business/ageism-advertising-aarp.html; and Ken Dychtwald, "Ageism Is Alive and Well in Advertising," AARP, September 8, 2021, https://www.aarp.org /work/working-at-50-plus/info-2021/ageism-in-advertising.html.

5. Monica Anderson and Andrew Perrin, "Technology Use Among Seniors," Pew Research Center, May 17, 2017, www.pewresearch.org/internet/2017/05/17/technology -use-among-seniors.

6. Joseph F. Coughlin, "Old Age Is Made Up—and This Concept Is Hurting Everyone," *MIT Technology Review*, August 21, 2019, https://www.technologyreview .com/2019/08/21/75537/old-age-is-made-upand-this-concept-is-hurting-everyone/.

7. Corinne Purtill, "The Key to Marketing to Older People? Don't Say 'Old,'" *New York Times*, December 8, 2021, https://www.nytimes.com/2021/12/08/business /dealbook/marketing-older-people.html.

8. H. Hershfield and L. L. Carstensen, "Your Messaging to Older Audiences Is Outdated," hbr.org, July 2, 2021, https://store.hbr.org/product/your-messaging -to-older-audiences-is-outdated/H06G88.

9. Rina Raphael, "Be a Friend to the Elderly, Get Paid," *New York Times*, April 27, 2020, https://www.nytimes.com/2020/04/23/style/companion-elderly-aid-friend .html.

10. Katherine Linzer, Binata Ray, and Navjot Singh, "Planning for an Aging Population," McKinsey.com, McKinsey Global Institute, July 31, 2020; Richard Dobbs, James Manyika, Jonathan Woetzel, Jaana Remes, Jesko Perrey, Greg Kelly, Kanaka Pattabiraman, and Hemant Sharma, "Urban World: The Global Consumers to Watch," McKinsey.com, McKinsey Global Institute, March 30, 2016.

11. Jaan Remes, Markus Schmid, and Monica Toriello, "Getting to Know Urban Elderly Consumers," *McKinsey Podcast*, November 29, 2016.

12. Juliette Cubanski, Wyatt Koma, Anthony Damico, and Tricia Neuman, "How Many Seniors Live in Poverty?" Kaiser Family Foundation, November 19, 2018, www .kff.org/report-section/how-many-seniors-live-in-poverty-issue-brief/.

13. Hsu, "Older People Are Ignored in Ageist Marketing"; and Jeff Beer, "Why Is Marketing to Seniors So Terrible," *Fast Company*, May 6, 2019, medium. com/fast-company/why-marketing-to-seniors-is-so-terrible.

Chapter 6

1. Daniel H. Pink, *To Sell Is Human: The Surprising Truth About Moving Others* (New York: Riverhead Books, 2013).

2. Julie Jargon, "How to Care for Aging Parents When You Can't Be There," *Wall Street Journal*, January 9, 2021, https://www.wsj.com/articles/how-to-care -for-aging-parents-when-you-cant-be-there-11610200808.

3. Susan Golden et al., "Landscape of Caregiving Innovations," Stanford Distinguished Careers Institute, September 2021, pp. 35–55, https://dci.stanford.edu/wp -content/uploads/2021/11/Landscape-of-Caregiving-Innovations-Report-1.pdf.

4. Robert Barba, "Best Buy to Acquire Jitterbug Parent GreatCall for $800 Million," *Wall Street Journal*, August 15, 2018, https://www.wsj.com/articles/best-buy-to -acquire-jitterbug-parent-greatcall-for-800-million-1534371246#:~:text=Robert%20 Barba,-Biography&text=BBY%201.79%25%20has%20agreed%20to,which%20 acquired%20GreatCall%20last%20year.

5. Paul J. Masotti, Robert Fick, Ana Johnson-Masotti, and Stuart MacLeod, "Healthy Naturally Occurring Retirement Communities: A Low-Cost Approach to Facilitating Healthy Aging," *American Journal of Public Health* 96, no. 7 (2006): 1164–1170.

6. Dan Buettner, *The Blue Zones: 9 Lesson for Living Longer from the People Who've Lived the Longest* (Washington, DC: National Geographic, 2012). See also www.bluezones.com.

7. For example, Massachusetts Healthy Aging Collaborative, https://mahealthyagingcollaborative.org, and the Center for Healthy Aging/New York Academy of Medicine, www.nyam.org.

8. World Health Organization, "Ageing: Healthy Ageing and Functional Ability," October 26, 2020, https://www.who.int/news-room/questions-and-answers/item /ageing-healthy-ageing-and-functional-ability.

9. The Mayo Clinic, "Healthy Lifestyle: Caregivers," www.mayoclinic.org /healthy-lifestyle.

10. Lorraine Morley, "AgeTech Investment: There Is Everything to Play For," *Longevity Technology*, August 18, 2020, https://www.longevity.technology/agetech -investment-there-is-everything-to-play-for/.

11. The Holding Co. and Pivotal Ventures, "Investor's Guide to the Care Economy: Four Dynamic Areas of Growth, " 2021, https://www.investin.care/; and Golden et al., "Landscape of Caregiving Innovations."

12. Think Tank: The New 3rd Age, "The Good Life in the 3rd Age," PFA, Denmark, January 1, 2018, https://pfa.dk/-/media/pfa-v2/dansk/dokumenter/kampagner /bn6427tanketankscenarierapportpixiendtp3lr.pdf.

Chapter 7

1. Morgan Borer, "Venture Capital Pioneer Alan Patricof and Wellness Executive Abby Miller Levy Launch Primetime Partners," *Business Wire*, July 29, 2020, https://www.businesswire.com/news/home/20200729005715/en/Venture-Capital-Pioneer -Alan-Patricof-and-Wellness-Executive-Abby-Miller-Levy-Launch-Primetime-Partners.

2. Joseph F. Coughlin, *The Longevity Economy: Unlocking the World's Fastest-Growing, Most Misunderstood Market* (New York: PublicAffairs, 2017).

3. Kerby Meres, "Entrepreneurs of a Certain Age, in This Uncertain Time," Currents, Kauffman Foundation, August 5, 2020, www.kauffman.org/currents /entrepreneurs-of-a-certain-age-uncertain-time.

4. Robert Chess, quoted in Reshma Kapadia, "Aging Is the Next Booming Business," *Barron's*, December 16, 2020, https://www.barrons.com/articles/looking-for -the-next-big-thing-it-may-be-catering-to-our-rapidly-aging-population-51608035401.

5. J. Glasner, "Funding Surges for Startups Serving Older Adults," *Crunchbase*, June 4, 2021, https://news.crunchbase.com/news/eldercare-senior-home-care -startups-funding/.

6. Interview with Lynn Herrick, COO, Best Buy Health, December 2021.

Chapter 8

1. S. Jay Olshansky, Daniel Perry, Richard A. Miller, and Robert N. Butler, "Pursuing the Longevity Dividend: Scientific Goals for an Aging World," *Annals NY Academy of Science* 1144, no. 1 (2007): 11–13.

2. Joe Kita, "Age Discrimination Still Thrives in America," AARP, December 30, 2019, www.aarp.org/work/working-at-50-plus/info-2019/age-discrimination-in -america.html.

3. Mercer, "Are You Age-Ready?," 2019, https://www.mercer.com/our -thinking/next-stage-are-you-age-ready.html; Transamerica Institute, "Age Friendly Workplace Programs: Recruiting and Retaining Experienced Employees," 2021, https://www.transamericainstitute.org/workplace-employers/age-friendly -workplaces; and AARP, "Disrupt Aging Initiatives," https://www.aarp.org /disrupt-aging.

4. Paul Irving, "When No One Retires," *Harvard Business Review*, November 7, 2018, https://hbr.org/2018/11/when-no-one-retires.

5. AARP, "Employer Pledge Program: Demonstrate Your Commitment to Experienced Workers," www.aarp.org/work/job-search/employer-pledge-companies.

6. AARP International, "Living, Learning and Earning Longer: How Modern Employers Should Embrace Longevity, a Collaboration from AARP, OECD, World Economic Forum," AARP International, December 2020, https://www.aarpinternational .org/initiatives/future-of-work/living-learning-and-earning-longer; Stuart Lewis, "Why Age Inclusive Workforces Play a Crucial Role in Building Back a Better Society

Post-COVID," World Economic Forum and OECD, September 7, 2021; and Decade of Healthy Ageing, "Global Campaign to Combat Ageism Through the Ages," https://www.decadeofhealthyageing.org/topics-initiatives/decade-action-areas /combatting-ageism.

7. Julie Sweetland, Andrew Volmert, and Moira O'Neil, "Finding the Frame: An Empirical Approach to Reframing Aging and Ageism," FrameWorks Institute, February 2017, www.frameworksinstitute.org/wp-content/uploads/2020/05/aging _research_report_final_2017.pdf.

8. Reframing Ageism Campaign, San Francisco, 2019, endageism.com.

9. A. Martin and M. S. North, "Equality for (Almost) All: Egalitarian Advocacy Predicts Lower Endorsement for Sexism and Racism, but Not Ageism," *Journal of Personality and Social Psychology*, January 18, 2021.

10. Michelle Singletary, "Retirement 'Baby Bonds' Could Help Close the Racial Wealth Gap," *Washington Post*, January 29, 2021, https://www.washingtonpost.com /business/2021/01/29/retirement-baby-bonds-racial-wealth-gap/.

11. Melinda French Gates, "Our Economy Is Powered by Caregivers; That's Why It's Time for National Paid Leave," *Time*, September 20, 2021, https://time.com /6098412/melinda-french-gates-paid-leave/.

12. California Department of Aging, "California's Master Plan for Aging," State of California, January 2021, www.aging.ca.gov/download.ashx?lE0rcNUV0zZe1bBmXl uFyg%3d%3d.

13. From California Department of Aging, "California's Master Plan for Aging."

14. Chip Conley, *Wisdom@ Work: The Making of a Modern Elder* (New York: Currency, 2018).

15. Joseph F. Coughlin and Luke Yoquinto, "Can Boston Be the Silicon Valley of Longevity?," *Boston Globe*, February 15, 2021, https://www.bostonglobe.com /2021/02/18/opinion/can-boston-be-silicon-valley-longevity/.

INDEX

ACKNOWLEDGMENTS

On June 12, 2015, I received a letter from the Stanford Distinguished Careers Institute (DCI) inviting me to be a Fellow in the 2016 class. A few hours earlier that day, I had attended my youngest child's high school graduation. At the same time that she was about to enter her launch stage during the first quarter of her life (Q1), I was about to enter my repurposing, continuous learning, and relaunching stages during my Q3. As she became a freshman in college, I became a freshman in the DCI.

Receiving that letter and participating in the DCI fellowship was one of the greatest life-changing events that I could have ever imagined at this stage of life. I am indebted to Phil Pizzo, the Founding Director of the DCI, for providing me with that opportunity and the many other opportunities that followed from being part of the DCI and Stanford community. Phil is a true scholar in many fields, a visionary, and the ultimate teacher. Even during my interview, he introduced me to the concept of longevity and how longer lives will affect careers, work, and the importance of living and dying with dignity. Phil also embodies the unique mindset at Stanford—what I refer to as the "yes and . . ." approach—and supported so many of my ideas for developing new initiatives.

Four years after I received that letter, and while I was traveling with that same daughter to celebrate her graduation from college, I received a phone call from Scott Berinato, senior editor at Harvard Business Review Press. Scott informed me that the book idea we had been discussing was approved by the Press's review team. Another new stage was about to begin for me, as I entered the portfolio stage of my life. Writing this book was the culmination of much of what I had learned during my fellowship at Stanford, and the effort drew on my prior work in public health, venture capital, and my own life experiences. Scott was uniquely able to take the enormous opportunities presented by longevity and help me distill it into eight chapters as a guide for future entrepreneurs intrigued by the opportunities that hundred-year lives present. He has insights about what should be shared and what should be left in the "parking lot." It has been a great joy to work with him and his team. Thank you for that phone call in the summer of 2019.

During my DCI fellowship, I also discovered the important work of the Stanford Center on Longevity, whose mission captivated me: SCL is designing a vision for hundred-year lives. I am so grateful to Laura Carstensen, the Founder and Director of SCL, who invited me to be its first visiting scholar after I completed my DCI fellowship. The optimism and positivity that Laura researches and exudes is infectious; I was inspired to consider how SCL's research could be applied to innovations. It wasn't just our better health and longer life expectancy that inspired and intrigued me. What I found so compelling is the question of what we would do with these extra years of life. And how could we continue to stay healthy for the remaining years, so as not to be in and out of hospitals as my parents had been?

My time at the center resulted in my codeveloping a new course with Laura Carstensen and Rob Chess. I had taken Rob's course, Innovation and Management in Health Care, while I was a DCI Fellow, and he was, and is, one of the very best teachers I have ever had. After discussing with Rob the enormous business implications and opportunities longevity presented, he was persuaded to plan and teach the new course. Working with Laura and Rob on developing a new course at Stanford was thrilling, where the focus is on what would most benefit the student. The course is in its third year of being offered at the Stanford Graduate School of Business, where I am now a lecturer in management. I continue to learn from Rob and Laura and, most significantly, from the students in the class.

One of the unique parts of the DCI fellowship is the special community that has emerged. One day during my fellowship, I sent an email to my group of fellows and partners, and asked if anyone wanted to meet for breakfast and talk about innovations for longevity. More than half my class showed up. This first gathering led to all sorts of wonderful meetings and evolved into a special interest group that now has more than eighty-five members from the eight DCI classes. From this group emerged an initiative, called dciX, which I now direct. To all the members of the Longevity Innovations Special Interest Group and dciX, I thank you for sharing your passion for this topic with me, brainstorming during our workshops, and constantly sharing articles, new companies, and new ideas.

Heartfelt gratitude to all the companies, entrepreneurs, and thought leaders I have interviewed over the past years; thank you for sharing your stories and challenges along the way. Your work is making it better for all of us to live healthy longer lives. Neil Blumenthal, Arthur Brettschneider, Darin Buxbaum, Suelin Chen, Carol Fishman Cohen, Joe Coughlin, Richard Eisenberg, Jeannine English, Keren Etkin, Katy Fike, Marc Freedman, James Fuccione, Mary Furlong, Lynn Herrick, Yossi Heyman, Carol Hymowitz, Paul Irving, Stephen Johnston, Randy Klein, Surya Koluri, Steve Pantilat, Lindsay Jurist-Rosner, Jake Rothstein, Jack Rowe, Stephen Schoenbaum, Andrew Scoot, Andy Sieg, Mark Silverman, Jay Newton Small, Jenny Xia Spradling, Seth Sternberg, Anne Tumlinson, Rob Urstein, Steve Wardle, Patty White, Julie Wroblewski, and Joy Zhang.

I am also very grateful to Pivotal Ventures, the Melinda French Gates investment and incubation company, for their invitation to join their initiatives on caregiving for older adults. Working with their caregiving team, Jennifer Stybel and Lara Jeremeko, and the Techstars Future of Longevity Accelerator led by Keith Camhi, has been one of the most purposeful and meaningful projects I have engaged with in my career.

Over the past five years, I have pestered all my friends with questions about what they want to be called and how they are living their lives, and I have learned how important it is to keep these connections. I will now stop asking if you want to be called elderly, or senior, or older, but I will not stop asking to get together. Special thanks to Sam Cuddeback, Marc Morgenstern, and Evie Sylvia, for sharing your insights with me.

My "Core Four" patiently waited while I emersed myself in writing this book, with most of the family room taken over with this project. Did you know that a ping-pong table makes a great desk when you are working from home? Dinners were filled with my trying out ideas on them, and their many contributions are reflected in the book as well. Thank you for always being my source of support, love, and laughter.

I started my career in public health, largely because I learned that many of the known causes of my father's multiple heart attacks and early death were preventable. Early on, I became passionate about how to prevent disease and serious illnesses—in both the public and the private sector. My mother's experiences as she began to decline, and the sorrow I felt at not being able to prevent her suffering, have also influenced my interests in addressing how older adults should be treated and cared for with dignity as a critical need in this country. My parents were my greatest teachers.

Approaching life with a mindset of growth and optimism is essential for longevity. That has been reinforced during the journey I had in writing this book. I feel so fortunate that my life is filled with many exciting stages for which I am most grateful. I hope yours will be too.

ABOUT THE AUTHOR

SUSAN WILNER GOLDEN is an expert on innovation and the unique entrepreneurial opportunities that longer lives and the growing $22 trillion longevity economy present. She teaches at the Stanford Graduate School of Business, and is the director of the dciX impact initiative at the Stanford Distinguished Careers Institute. Golden also serves as Mentor-in-Residence to the Techstars Future of Longevity Accelerator, and as a thought-leader partner with Pivotal Ventures on their caregiving innovation and investment initiatives. She is an adviser to startups and companies on their longevity strategies.

Her career includes time spent in venture capital, public health, and life sciences, which provides her with a multidimensional, multidisciplinary perspective on longevity opportunities. Golden is herself an example of Stage (Not Age) thinking, and is living a multistage life. She received a doctorate in science from the Harvard T.H. Chan School of Public Health, attended Harvard Business School's program in management development, and was a 2016 Stanford Distinguished Careers Institute fellow.